AF480665

The Safavid Empire

The Rise, Fall, and Enduring Legacy of the Dynasty That Made Modern Iran

Samuel Corwin

Table Of Contents

Introduction:

The Empire That Made Iran

In 1501, a fourteen-year-old warrior-mystic with auburn hair and a turban crowned by twelve crimson folds rode into Tabriz and declared himself Shah. Within a generation, he and his successors would invent a country that still bears their imprint five hundred years later.

His name was Ismail, and the headgear his followers wore - the *taj*, twelve scarlet pleats honoring the Twelve Imams of Shi'a Islam - gave them a name the Turks spat like a curse: Qizilbash, the Red Heads. They were cavalrymen, holy warriors, and devotees of a Sufi master whose ancestors had built a quiet religious lodge in the town of Ardabil two centuries earlier. Now that lodge had become an army, and the army had become a kingdom. Ismail, riding into the old Aqquyunlu capital in the wreckage of a defeated dynasty, did something unprecedented. He proclaimed Twelver Shi'ism the official faith of his realm, in a region that was overwhelmingly Sunni, and he ordered the first Friday sermon in his name to curse the first three caliphs revered by the Sunni majority. It was an act of breathtaking audacity. It was also the founding gesture of modern Iran. Over the next 235 years, the dynasty Ismail launched would forge a state, a sect, a culture, and a self-image that outlasted the Safavids themselves and continues to shape one of the most consequential nations of our century.

Why the Safavids Still Matter

Ask most Western readers to name an Iranian dynasty and they will usually reach for the Achaemenids of Cyrus and Darius, or perhaps the Sasanians who fought Rome to a standstill. The Safavids, who came after both by more than a thousand years, get short shrift. This is a mistake. The Iran of today - its borders, its dominant religion, its bureaucratic instincts, its uneasy mixture of Persian high culture and Turkic military tradition, its sense of itself as a singular civilization wedged between hostile neighbors - was not bequeathed by the ancients. It was built between 1501 and 1736 by a family of former Sufi sheikhs and the soldiers, scholars, painters, and merchants who served them.

Consider what the Safavids made permanent. Before Ismail, Iran was a geographical expression. Its plateau had been ruled in pieces by Mongols, Timurids, Turkmen confederations, and local strongmen. There was no political unit called Iran in the modern sense, no single sovereign claiming the whole plateau as a coherent realm. After the Safavids, there was. They drew the rough outline that survives on maps today. They gave it a capital tradition - first Tabriz, then Qazvin, then the splendor of Isfahan - and a court culture so dazzling that European ambassadors went home babbling about gardens, tilework, and silk.

More consequentially still, they made Iran Shi'a. In 1500, perhaps a tenth of the population of the Iranian plateau followed the Twelver branch of Shi'ism. By 1700, the figure was approaching ninety percent. This was the largest forced - and in places persuaded - religious transformation in the early modern Islamic world. It produced a permanent fault line running through the heart of the Middle East, separating Shi'a Iran from Sunni Anatolia, Sunni Mesopotamia (until much later), and Sunni Central Asia. Every news cycle out of Beirut, Baghdad, Sanaa, or Bahrain still echoes that decision made in Tabriz five centuries ago.

The Safavids also bequeathed an idea: that political and religious authority in Iran are properly fused. The Shah was both king and the earthly shadow of the Hidden Imam, both warlord and saint. When Ayatollah Khomeini returned from exile in 1979 to establish a clerical republic, he was operating inside a political theology that the Safavids had spent two centuries constructing. One can trace a clear, if winding, line from Ismail's twelve-pleated turban to the *velayat-e faqih* of contemporary Tehran.

And then there is the art. The miniatures of Riza Abbasi, the carpets that ended up in Venetian palaces, the blue-tiled domes of Isfahan, the calligraphy, the poetry, the chronicles - the Safavids preside over one of the great cultural flowerings of human history, on par with Renaissance Florence or Ming Beijing. To ignore them is to amputate a limb from the body of world civilization.

A World Between Empires: Ottomans, Mughals, and the Safavid Middle

The Safavids did not arise in isolation. They were the middle child of a remarkable family of Islamic gunpowder empires that dominated Eurasia in the sixteenth century. To their west lay the Ottomans, sprawling from Algiers to Basra, custodians of Mecca and Medina, and self-appointed champions of Sunni orthodoxy. To their east, beginning in 1526, rose the Mughals of India, Persianate in their court culture, fabulously wealthy, and religiously eclectic. The Safavids were smaller than either, poorer than the Mughals, and militarily outmatched by the Ottomans. Yet they shaped both.

The Ottoman-Safavid rivalry was the defining geopolitical contest of the western Islamic world for two centuries. It began catastrophically for Ismail. In 1514, on the plain of Chaldiran in eastern Anatolia, Sultan Selim I's disciplined Janissaries and field artillery shredded the Qizilbash cavalry. The young Shah, who had until then believed himself supernaturally invincible, watched his army break and his harem fall into Ottoman hands. He never led troops in person again. The trauma of Chaldiran haunted Safavid strategy for the rest of the dynasty's existence and forced its rulers, eventually, to professionalize an army that could meet gunpowder with gunpowder.

To the east, the Mughals were less rival than reluctant cousin. Babur, founder of the Mughal line, had taken refuge with Shah Ismail before his Indian conquests; his son Humayun was rescued from oblivion by Shah Tahmasp and returned to Delhi at the head of a Safavid-backed expedition. Persian was the language of the Mughal court, Persian poets and administrators flocked to Agra and Lahore, and Safavid artistic styles set the template for Mughal painting. The Safavids exported a culture that helped govern an India they never ruled.

This middle position - geographically squeezed, demographically smaller, religiously distinct - forced the Safavids to become inventive. They could not match Ottoman manpower or Mughal wealth. So they cultivated diplomacy with European powers eager for an ally against the Sultan, mastered the silk trade that connected Asia to Europe, and built an ideological identity so sharp that it gave a small state outsized weight.

The Central Question: How Does a Sufi Order Become a State?

At the heart of the Safavid story sits a puzzle that historians have wrestled with for a hundred years and that this book addresses head-on. How did a quietist mystical brotherhood, founded by a thirteenth-century Kurdish sheikh in a market town in Azerbaijan, transform itself in eight generations into one of the great empires of the early modern world? And, having done so, how did it then transform again - shedding its mystical roots, suppressing the very Sufi orders from which it had sprung, and reinventing itself as a sober Shi'a theocracy run by jurists and bureaucrats?

The Safavid order began with Sheikh Safi al-Din, who died in 1334. He was a respected but unremarkable Sunni Sufi master. His tomb complex at Ardabil drew pilgrims and donations. Over the next century and a half, his successors did something strange. They militarized. They began recruiting Turkmen tribesmen from eastern Anatolia and Syria - tough, restless, and hungry - and offered them not just spiritual instruction but a political program. Somewhere in the fifteenth century, the order also drifted toward an extreme form of Shi'ism that bordered on the heterodox. Sheikh Junayd and his son Haydar, Ismail's grandfather and father, fell in battle trying to carve out a principality for themselves. By the time fourteen-year-old Ismail emerged from hiding in 1499, the Safavid order was less a religious confraternity than a revolutionary insurgency with a charismatic boy at its head.

What happened next is the central drama of this book. Ismail's followers worshipped him - quite literally, as a divine incarnation. He wrote poetry in Turkish proclaiming himself the manifestation of God. After Chaldiran shattered the myth of his invincibility, his successors had to walk the religious revolution back without losing the political revolution it had enabled. They imported Shi'a clerics from Lebanon and Bahrain to teach a population that knew almost nothing about Twelver doctrine. They built madrasas. They patronized scholars who would, by the seventeenth century, claim authority independent of - and sometimes against - the Shah himself. They turned a heresy into an orthodoxy and, in doing so, planted the seeds of a clerical establishment that would outlive every Safavid king.

The transformation of order into state is the book's spine. Every chapter that follows is, in some sense, an attempt to answer it.

Scope, Sources, and Approach

This book covers the Safavid dynasty from Ismail's coronation in 1501 to the Afghan sack of Isfahan in 1722 and the rise of Nader Shah, who finally extinguished the last Safavid pretenders in 1736. Within that span, it ranges across politics, religion, military affairs, art, commerce, and daily life, though no single volume can do justice to all of it. The emphasis falls on questions of identity and institution-building: how a state was made, how a faith was imposed, and how both reshaped a people.

The sources are richer than many readers might expect. Safavid court chroniclers - Khwandamir, Iskandar Beg Munshi, and others - left voluminous if partisan accounts. European travelers from Anthony

Sherley to Jean Chardin and Engelbert Kaempfer recorded what they saw, often with sharp eyes and sharper prejudices. Persian poetry, royal correspondence, religious treatises, and the surviving architecture and miniatures all speak. So do Ottoman archives, Venetian diplomatic dispatches, and the records of the Dutch and English East India Companies, who built factories on the Persian Gulf.

This account leans on a generation of recent scholarship - the work of Roger Savory, Andrew Newman, Rudi Matthee, Kathryn Babayan, Sussan Babaie, and others - that has rescued the Safavids from the condescension of older narratives treating them as a decadent oriental interlude between the Mongols and the modern. Where historians genuinely disagree - about the depth of Ismail's messianic claims, about the causes of the seventeenth-century decline, about the role of Shi'a clerics in the dynasty's fall - the disagreements are flagged rather than smoothed over. The aim is a story that is honest about its uncertainties without losing its narrative drive.

A Roadmap of What Lies Ahead

The chapters that follow trace the Safavid arc from origins to aftermath. We begin in the mountains of Azerbaijan with Sheikh Safi al-Din and his quiet brotherhood, watching across two centuries as a Sufi order metamorphoses into a militant movement. We then ride into Tabriz with Ismail, witness the catastrophe of Chaldiran, and follow the long, cautious reign of Shah Tahmasp as he picks up the pieces and learns, painfully, that holy war alone cannot sustain a kingdom.

The middle of the book belongs to Shah Abbas the Great, who took a battered, fractious realm at the close of the sixteenth century and rebuilt it into something formidable. We walk the great square of Isfahan that he laid out, examine the slave-soldier corps with which he broke the power of the Qizilbash, and follow the Armenian merchants of New Julfa as they spun a silk-trade web from London to Manila. Subsequent chapters consider the rise of Shi'a clerical authority, the strange and brilliant world of Safavid art and architecture, the harem as

10

an institution of power, the empire's relations with Mughal India and tsarist Russia, and the slow rot of the seventeenth century.

The final movement covers the collapse: the Afghan invasion, the sack of Isfahan, the warlord Nader Shah's terrifying brief restoration, and the dynasty's strange afterlife in the political and religious imagination of Iran down to the present day. The question never strays far - how did a Sufi order become a state, and what kind of country did that state leave behind?

Quick Summary

- The Safavid Empire (1501-1736) created the political, religious, and cultural template of modern Iran.

- Founded by the fourteen-year-old Shah Ismail I, the dynasty grew out of a Sufi order from Ardabil that militarized over the fifteenth century.

- Ismail made Twelver Shi'ism the state religion in 1501, transforming a Sunni-majority region into the Shi'a heartland it remains today.

- The 1514 defeat at Chaldiran by the Ottomans punctured Safavid claims of invincibility and reshaped the dynasty's military and religious strategy.

- The Safavids occupied the geographic and cultural middle between the Ottoman and Mughal empires, exporting Persianate culture across Eurasia.

- Shah Abbas the Great (r. 1588-1629) refounded the empire, built Isfahan, and integrated it into global trade networks.

- The dynasty fell to Afghan invaders in 1722 but left a Shi'a clerical establishment and a sense of Iranian identity that have shaped the region ever since.

Five hundred years after a teenage mystic crowned himself in Tabriz, the country he conjured still answers in his accent. To understand Iran - its faith, its borders, its quarrels, its self-regard - one must understand the Safavids. That is where we now begin.

To understand the boy who rode into Tabriz, we have to understand what rode in with him: two centuries of accumulated holiness, of land bequeathed to a lodge, of disciples who had learned to call a sheikh's word the word of God. Ismail did not invent the authority he wielded at fourteen. He inherited it, already polished by generations of ancestors who had transformed a provincial Sufi order into something closer to a dynasty-in-waiting. Before the crimson crown could be placed on a young head, a quieter crown had been shaped in Ardabil.

Chapter 1:

Ardabil's Holy Lineage

Before they wore crowns, the Safavids wore wool. Before they commanded cavalry, they counted prayer beads. And before their name thundered from Tabriz to Herat, it belonged to a quiet sheikh in a quiet town, whose followers came seeking not conquest but God.

The Safavid story does not begin in 1501 with a teenage warlord galloping into Tabriz. It begins more than two centuries earlier, in a provincial pilgrimage town in the hills near the Caspian, where a Sufi master named Safi al-Din attracted disciples, land, and a reputation for holiness that would outlive him by generations. The transformation of that lodge - a place of chant, charity, and ascetic withdrawal - into the nerve center of a militant dynasty is one of the most peculiar political metamorphoses in Islamic history. It took roughly two hundred years. It required the accidents of marriage, migration, and mysticism to align. And it ended with a boy king declaring himself the hidden incarnation of divine authority, at the head of an army of red-capped tribesmen who believed he could not die. To understand that improbable climax, we have to begin with the man who never intended any of it: a contemplative Sunni sheikh who taught that the true battle was with the self.

Sheikh Safi al-Din and the Founding of the Order

Safi al-Din Ardabili was born in 1253, four years before Hulagu Khan's Mongols sacked Baghdad and ended five centuries of Abbasid rule. He grew up in a world still reeling from that catastrophe. The great madrasas lay in ruins or reduced estate. Across the Iranian plateau, the formal institutions of Sunni orthodoxy were weak, and into that vacuum had poured something older and more supple: the Sufi brotherhoods, with their chains of spiritual masters, their lodges, their songs and ecstatic disciplines.

Ardabil, where Safi al-Din was born and would die, sat on the Caspian side of the Sabalan massif in Azerbaijan. A merchant town on the caravan road, cold in winter, cut through by pilgrim traffic heading to holy shrines, its inhabitants spoke Azeri Turkish in the bazaar and read Persian in the mosque. That bilingual, border-straddling character would mark the order Safi al-Din founded - and the empire his descendants would one day build.

As a young man, he set out to find a spiritual master. The accounts say he traveled to Shiraz hoping to study with a famous sheikh there, arrived to find him dead, and was redirected north to Gilan, where he entered the service of Sheikh Zahid al-Gilani. Zahid became his teacher, his father-in-law, and in time his predecessor at the head of a Sufi network that stretched across the Caucasus. Safi al-Din married Zahid's daughter and, on the old master's death around 1301, inherited leadership of the order.

Under his guidance it grew explosively. The Safaviyya - the order named for him - was, in its earliest phase, unambiguously Sunni, most likely following the Shafi'i school of law. It was also conventionally mystical: its teachings emphasized dhikr, the rhythmic remembrance of God; the purification of the soul; submission to the sheikh; and the renunciation of worldly entanglement. Safi al-Din was not a revolutionary. He was a spiritual director of remarkable charisma, and men of all ranks came to him - peasants, merchants, Mongol officials, Ilkhanid emirs - seeking blessing, guidance, and intercession.

What made the Safaviyya different from dozens of comparable orders was not doctrine but organization. Safi al-Din and his successors built, around the lodge at Ardabil, an administrative machine: a network of deputies called khalifas sent out to recruit and to collect, regular flows of gifts from disciples in distant provinces, a ledger of the faithful, a chain of command. The order was a confraternity, but it was also, already, a kind of state in miniature.

When Safi al-Din died in 1334, at the age of eighty-one, he was buried in Ardabil beside his master Zahid's tomb. His son Sadr al-Din inherited the sheikhship. Hagiography soon gathered around the founder's memory - miracle stories, healing tales, a sanitized genealogy that would eventually claim descent from the seventh Shi'i Imam, Musa al-Kazim, and through him from the Prophet Muhammad himself. That claim was almost certainly a later fabrication, retrofitted when the family's politics shifted. In Safi al-Din's own lifetime, no one seems to have suggested it. He was a holy man of Kurdish or Iranian stock, venerated not for his blood but for his sanctity.

Yet from that sanctity his descendants would, within five generations, manufacture a throne.

The Lodge at Ardabil: Piety, Patronage, and Pilgrimage

For two centuries, the physical heart of the Safavid phenomenon was a walled compound on the edge of Ardabil. Pilgrims approached it through gardens and courtyards arranged in a processional sequence designed to slow the visitor, quiet the mind, and focus attention on the shrine at the center: the tomb tower of Sheikh Safi, its interior dense with glazed tile, carved plaster, and hanging lamps. Around it clustered a mosque, a refectory for the poor, a hospice for travelers, a library, kitchens, and the houses of the sheikh's family and retainers.

This complex was not a passive monument. It was an economic engine. Over the fourteenth and fifteenth centuries, successive Safavid sheikhs accumulated enormous waqf endowments - pious foundations of land, orchards, mills, bazaars, and villages whose revenues were legally bound to the shrine. Mongol and post-Mongol rulers, eager to buy blessing and legitimacy from a prestigious holy family, contributed liberally. The Ilkhans exempted the order from taxation. Timur is said to have visited Ardabil and, in a famous gesture, released Anatolian captives at the sheikh's request. Each concession added to the lodge's wealth and reach.

What flowed into Ardabil was not only money but men. Pilgrims came from Syria, from eastern Anatolia, from the Caucasus and the Iranian plateau. Many stayed. Those who left went home bearing a loyalty to the sheikh that could be reactivated decades later. By the mid-fifteenth century, the Safavid order had become something no mere Sufi brotherhood in the region could match: a transnational confraternity with tens of thousands of committed disciples spread across rival kingdoms.

The shrine also served as a mausoleum dynasty. Sheikh after sheikh was buried in and around Safi al-Din's tomb, reinforcing the impression that the family itself - its blood, its line - carried a concentrated sanctity. Later, when Shah Tahmasp expanded the complex in the 1530s, he did so in part to make this genealogical claim architecturally unmistakable. He commissioned the porcelain house, which held a royal collection of Chinese ceramics given as votive offerings. He commissioned the pair of colossal knotted-pile carpets now known as the Ardabil Carpets, one of which survives in the Victoria and Albert Museum in London, the other in the Los Angeles County Museum of Art. Sixteen feet by thirty-four, with some twenty-five million knots between them, they are among the most ambitious textiles ever woven. Their inscription, a couplet by the poet Hafiz, frames a hanging lamp at the center of an infinite medallion field - a carpet that is also a prayer.

Those carpets belonged to a later moment, when Safavid sheikhs had become Safavid kings. But they pointed backward as much as forward. They were meant to honor the founder, to anchor the dynasty's authority in his tomb, and to remind every visitor who entered the shrine that the sovereign of Iran drew his legitimacy not merely from conquest but from the uninterrupted holiness of this particular bloodline, radiating from this particular grave.

For two centuries before the Ardabil Carpets were woven, though, that bloodline had been quietly accumulating another kind of capital: followers willing to fight.

From Sunni Sufism to Shi'i Militancy

At some point during the fifteenth century, the Safavid order changed. It acquired an army. It adopted a new theology. It turned from the cultivation of inward serenity toward the promise of apocalyptic struggle. Historians have argued for generations about when and why this happened, and the sources are frustratingly thin. But the broad shape is clear.

The first shift was sectarian. The early Safaviyya was Sunni. By the later fifteenth century it was recognizably Shi'i, and by 1501 it was militantly so - specifically, Twelver Shi'i, venerating the twelve Imams descended from Ali and awaiting the return of the hidden Twelfth. Why the change? The Iranian plateau in this period was a place where sectarian boundaries blurred. Popular piety across Anatolia and Azerbaijan already wove together devotion to Ali, reverence for the family of the Prophet, and folk beliefs about returning messiahs and incarnations of divinity. This diffuse constellation of loyalties, sometimes called Alid loyalism, was not yet orthodox Twelver Shi'ism, but it provided fertile soil for leaders who wished to claim something more than ordinary sainthood.

The Safavid sheikhs accelerated that process by revising their own family history. Somewhere in the generations after Safi al-Din, official genealogies began to insist that the founder descended from Musa al-Kazim, the seventh Shi'i Imam. The claim fused spiritual lineage with bloodline in a way orthodox Sunnism could not accommodate. If the sheikh of Ardabil was a descendant of the Imams, then obedience to him was not merely pious. It was obligatory. It had eschatological stakes.

The second shift was social. Through the fifteenth century, the order's center of gravity migrated from urban Ardabil outward to rural, tribal, largely Turkmen-speaking populations in eastern Anatolia, northern Syria, and the Caucasus. These were pastoralists and nomadic warriors - men for whom the settled orthodoxies of the lawyer and the madrasa held little authority, and for whom a charismatic sheikh promising divine favor and booty held a great deal. They were the discontented of the post-Mongol steppe frontier, chafing under the Ottoman advance in the west and the decaying Turkmen confederations in the east.

The third shift was generational. Junayd, who became head of the order around 1447, was the grandfather of Shah Ismail, and he is the figure around whom the transformation crystallized. He was expelled from Ardabil by his uncle - a reminder that the family itself was divided over what it was becoming - and spent years in exile wandering among his Turkmen devotees. During those wanderings he reportedly began to accept, or perhaps to encourage, veneration of himself not merely as sheikh but as something approaching a divine figure. Contemporary chroniclers hostile to the Safavids complained that his followers called him God. Whether or not Junayd said so himself, his devotees clearly did.

This is the crucial mutation. Traditional Sufism taught that the disciple should annihilate his ego in the being of his sheikh, who in turn was annihilated in God. Stretch that doctrine far enough, in the hands of ecstatic and unlettered tribesmen, and the sheikh becomes a window onto divinity - then a doorway - then, eventually, a door that has fused with what lies beyond it. By the time Junayd's grandson Ismail composed his Turkish-language poetry under the pen name Khata'i, he was writing lines in which he effectively identified himself with God, with Ali, and with the hidden Imam - all at once.

Orthodox Shi'i clerics would later find this deeply embarrassing. Once the Safavids held Iran, they imported sober jurists from Lebanon and Bahrain to teach their subjects a properly scholastic Twelver

Shi'ism and to quietly bury the more extravagant theology that had won them the throne. But in the fifteenth century, that extravagance was the fuel. Men were willing to die - and, more importantly, to kill - for a sheikh who was God's shadow on earth. Nobody died for a scholar of jurisprudence.

The Aq Qoyunlu Marriage and the Inheritance of Anatolia

The Safavids did not acquire their empire by theology alone. They acquired it, in part, the old-fashioned way: through a well-placed marriage.

By the mid-fifteenth century, the dominant power in western Iran and eastern Anatolia was the Aq Qoyunlu, the confederation of the White Sheep Turkmens, whose greatest ruler, Uzun Hasan, assembled a state that stretched from Baghdad to the edges of Khorasan. Uzun Hasan was a shrewd diplomat as well as a formidable cavalry commander. He corresponded with Venice about joint action against the Ottomans. He entertained European envoys at Tabriz. And he understood that the Safavid sheikhs, with their network of Turkmen devotees, were simultaneously a valuable ally and a dangerous rival.

His response was to bind them to his house. He gave his sister Khadija Begum in marriage to Sheikh Junayd, despite the sheikh's questionable orthodoxy and his growing militancy. Then, a generation later, he gave his own daughter Martha - also known by her Muslim name, Alamshah Begum - to Junayd's son Haydar. Martha herself was half-Byzantine, her mother a Trebizond princess from the last imperial remnant of the Greek east. The child of that second marriage would be Ismail.

Consider that bloodline. Ismail carried in his veins the Sufi sheikhs of Ardabil, the warrior khans of the White Sheep, and the last Christian emperors of Trebizond. He was a compound of the mystical, the nomadic, and the imperial. When he presented himself to his followers as the rightful lord of Iran, he could point to more overlapping legitimacies than any rival in the region.

The marriage also transferred something less tangible but more practical: a political inheritance. When the Aq Qoyunlu confederation collapsed in civil war in the 1490s, large segments of its Turkmen manpower - tribes that had fought for Uzun Hasan and his heirs - were suddenly available. Many of them were already Safavid devotees, or their kinsmen were. The young Ismail, through his Aq Qoyunlu mother, could present himself as a legitimate claimant to the loyalties those tribes had previously owed to her family. The line between Aq Qoyunlu and Safavid soldiery began to dissolve.

The Safavids thus inherited not only a theology of holy war but also a standing pool of experienced cavalry looking for a new leader. The Aq Qoyunlu had provided them, unintentionally, with the raw material of an army. All that remained was to forge it.

Junayd, Haydar, and the Rise of the Qizilbash

That forging was the work of two generations and cost both leaders their lives.

Junayd transformed the order into a militant movement during his years of exile among the Turkmen tribes. In 1460 he led a raiding expedition into the Caucasus, ostensibly a ghaza or holy war against Christian Circassians, but really a test of his ability to command armed followers in the field. He was killed in battle against the forces of the Shirvanshah, the regional Muslim ruler whose lands he had violated. The death of a sheikh on the battlefield might, in another order, have ended the experiment. Among the Safavids it did the opposite. Junayd became a martyr. His son Haydar inherited both the order and the blood feud.

Haydar was the innovator of the uniform. Around him, his Turkmen followers began wearing a distinctive headgear: a tall crimson cap with twelve folds or gores, each representing one of the Twelve Imams. It was at once a religious statement, a tribal marker, and a declaration of allegiance. The Ottomans and their Turkmen rivals began calling these men Qizilbash, Turkish for "red heads." The name stuck. In time it would be worn as a badge of pride by the cavalry who conquered Iran, and as a term of fear by everyone they conquered.

Haydar also consummated the Aq Qoyunlu alliance by marrying Martha and fathering Ismail. But like his father, he pushed too far, too fast. In 1488 he led his Qizilbash warriors north on another expedition of holy raiding, and like his father, he was killed by the Shirvanshah. The family's quarrels with Shirvan were becoming an inherited liability.

Haydar's sons were hunted. The eldest, Ali, was killed a few years later by Aq Qoyunlu rivals who finally grasped what the Safavids were becoming. The youngest, Ismail, was hidden away in Gilan, in the mountainous Caspian province, where sympathetic local rulers kept him alive through his childhood. He emerged in 1499, barely twelve years old, to claim the leadership of the order and summon the Qizilbash.

They came. By the summer of 1500, seven thousand of them had gathered around him at Erzincan in eastern Anatolia - Turkmen cavalry from a dozen tribes, bound by oaths of devotion to a boy they regarded as a living manifestation of the divine. Within a year Ismail would defeat the Shirvanshah who had killed his father and grandfather, avenge three generations of grievance, and ride into Tabriz as shah. The Sufi lodge at Ardabil had produced a conqueror.

Key Figures & Events

- **Safi al-Din Ardabili (1253-1334)**: founder of the Safaviyya order, a Sunni Sufi master whose descendants would claim him as the root of a sacred dynasty.

- **Sheikh Junayd (d. 1460)**: grandfather of Shah Ismail; transformed the order into a militant movement and died raiding in the Caucasus.

- **Sheikh Haydar (d. 1488)**: son of Junayd, husband of an Aq Qoyunlu princess, creator of the twelve-gored red cap from which the Qizilbash took their name.

- **Uzun Hasan (r. 1453-1478)**: Aq Qoyunlu ruler who tied the Safavids to his house through marriage, inadvertently equipping them with imperial legitimacy.

- **The Ardabil shrine complex**: two centuries of accumulated land, waqf, and devotion, expanded dramatically under Shah Tahmasp in the 1530s.

Analysis

The rise of the Safavids confounds easy explanation because it depended on the fusion of forces that rarely combine. A quietist Sufi order acquired, through the accidents of family and geography, a following among precisely the population - nomadic Turkmen - most receptive to charismatic, messianic, warrior leadership. A family of Sunni sheikhs discovered that a Shi'i reinvention of their lineage dramatically sharpened the claims they could make on that following. A marriage alliance with the Aq Qoyunlu opened access to professional cavalry and imperial precedent. And two martyred sheikhs gave the movement the moral capital of vengeance.

None of these ingredients was unique to Ardabil. Sufi orders with political ambitions existed across the Islamic world. Messianic expectation was ubiquitous in the fifteenth century. Sectarian boundaries blurred everywhere on the Anatolian-Iranian frontier. But only at Ardabil did they combine in the right proportions and at the right time. By 1500, the Safavid family had assembled a package - genealogical, theological, military, matrimonial - that no rival could match. What remained was to use it.

The deeper significance is that the dynasty which would define Iran for two centuries, and shape its religious identity to the present day, did not begin as a state. It began as a church, in the broadest sense: a community of belief. When Ismail rode into Tabriz in 1501, he was not founding a government on the model of the sultanates around him. He was elevating a sacred order into sovereignty. That origin would mark everything that followed - the strange cult of personality around the shah, the fusion of crown and clergy, the messianic streak that lingered in Iranian politics long after the Safavids themselves had fallen.

Quick Summary

- The Safavid dynasty began not as a state but as the Safaviyya, a Sufi order founded in Ardabil by Sheikh Safi al-Din (1253-1334).

- Originally Sunni and mystical, the order accumulated vast landed endowments and a transnational network of disciples across two centuries.

- During the fifteenth century, the order shifted toward militant Shi'ism, claiming descent from the Imams and attracting nomadic Turkmen warriors.

- Strategic marriages with the Aq Qoyunlu Turkmen confederation gave the family imperial legitimacy and, eventually, access to its cavalry.

- Sheikhs Junayd (d. 1460) and Haydar (d. 1488) transformed the order into an armed movement; both died fighting the Shirvanshah.

- Haydar's followers adopted the red twelve-gored cap that gave them their name: the Qizilbash.

- Haydar's son Ismail emerged from hiding in 1499, rallied 7,000 Qizilbash at Erzincan, and by 1501 had conquered Tabriz.

- The Safavid state was born as a sacralized dynasty, founded on the conviction that its ruler carried divine authority through blood.

From a windswept lodge beside the Caspian, an army had marched out to claim the Iranian plateau. The boy at its head believed - or allowed his followers to believe - that he was something more than a king. What he would do with that conviction, and what Iran would do with him, is the story of the next chapter.

Seven thousand Qizilbash at Erzincan, a boy at their head who believed - or was willing to let them believe - that he carried divinity in his blood. The inheritance from Ardabil had matured into an army, and the army was already moving. What followed was not the slow consolidation of a provincial warlord but something stranger and faster: a thirteen-year-old emerging from the forests of Gilan and, within a decade, welding the Iranian plateau into a single realm. The making of that realm, and the price exacted for it, is where the Safavid story turns from prophecy to conquest.

Chapter 2:

Ismail and the Conquest of Persia

He was thirteen when he emerged from hiding, fourteen when he took Tabriz, and twenty-three when he had welded most of Iran into a single realm. To his followers, Ismail was not merely a king but the long-awaited Mahdi.

No figure in Iranian history bursts onto the stage quite like Shah Ismail I. Born in 1487 into a bloodline already drenched in martyrdom, orphaned before he could walk, hunted through his boyhood by kings who understood exactly what he represented, he emerged from the damp forests of Gilan as a teenager at the head of a movement that would redraw the map of western Asia. Within a decade he had conquered an empire stretching from the Euphrates to the Oxus. Within two he had imposed upon it a religious identity - Twelver Shi'ism - that still defines Iran more than five centuries later. His story is part military biography, part messianic drama, and part the founding myth of a nation. To understand modern Iran one must begin with this boy-king, his devoted Turkmen horsemen, and the blend of sword and verse by which he made himself both shah and saint.

A Child in Hiding: The Years in Gilan

Ismail's childhood was a fugitive's childhood. His father, Shaykh Haydar, had transformed the Safavid Sufi order of Ardabil into a militant brotherhood, arming his disciples and crowning them with the distinctive twelve-gored crimson cap that would give them their name: the Qizilbash, the Red Heads. In 1488, Haydar was killed in battle against the Shirvanshah, the ruler of the Caspian principality of Shirvan, whose forces were backed by the dominant power of the region, the Aqqoyunlu - the White Sheep Turkmen confederation.

The infant Ismail was dangerous simply by existing. He was the grandson of Uzun Hasan, the great Aqqoyunlu sovereign, through his mother; he was the heir to Haydar's Sufi following through his father. Such a child, suspended between a dynasty and a congregation, could not be allowed to grow into a man. The Aqqoyunlu ruler Yaqub imprisoned Ismail and his brothers. When civil war tore through the Aqqoyunlu in the 1490s, the boys were freed, then hunted again. Ismail's elder brother Ali was killed in battle in 1494, reportedly after declaring that the leadership of the order would pass to seven-year-old Ismail.

What saved him was geography. Smuggled north by loyal disciples, Ismail was hidden in Lahijan, a town in the forested, rain-soaked province of Gilan along the Caspian. Gilan was a world unto itself - a humid jungle of rice paddies and silk villages walled off from the Iranian plateau by the Alborz mountains, ruled by a local Shi'ite lord named Karkiya Mirza Ali, who refused every demand to hand the boy over.

For roughly five years - from about 1494 to 1499 - Ismail lived in Lahijan as part student, part icon. Tutors drilled him in Arabic, Persian, and the Quran, and, crucially, in the theology of Twelver Shi'ism. He learned to read and compose poetry in his native Azeri Turkish. He also learned, day by day, that men he had never met were willing to die for him. Qizilbash emissaries slipped into Gilan from Anatolia, Syria, and Azerbaijan, pledging the loyalty of their clans - the Ustajlu, Shamlu, Rumlu, Tekelu, Afshar, Qajar, and others - to a child who had inherited the sanctity of four generations of Safavid shaykhs.

By the time Ismail was twelve, the calculation had flipped. He was no longer the hunted but the rising threat, and the Aqqoyunlu were fragmenting into rival courts at Tabriz and Baghdad. In the summer of 1499, he slipped out of Lahijan with a small band of followers and rode south toward Ardabil, the ancestral shrine-town of his order. The years in hiding were over. The years of war were about to begin.

The March on Tabriz, 1501

Ismail's opening campaign reads like something his own court poets might have invented. He set out with perhaps three hundred men. Within eighteen months he had ten thousand.

From Ardabil he moved first to Erzincan in eastern Anatolia, where the Qizilbash clans had been summoned to muster in the summer of 1500. The gathering was less an army assembling than a congregation answering a call. These were men who believed, many of them literally, that the boy they had come to serve was the incarnation of divine light passed down from Ali ibn Abi Talib, the first Shi'ite Imam. They fought, they said, not merely for land but for the return of justice to the world.

The first target was Shirvan - the kingdom that had killed Ismail's father. In the winter of 1500-1501, at a place called Jabani near the Caspian coast, Ismail's Qizilbash smashed the army of Farrukh Yasar, the Shirvanshah, who was hunted down and killed. Vengeance, that ancient engine of Turko-Iranian politics, had been served. It was also the first proof of concept: this boy could win battles.

Then came the opportunity that would make him an emperor. The Aqqoyunlu sultan Alvand, based at Tabriz, marched east to crush the upstart before he could consolidate. The two armies met in the summer of 1501 at Sharur, in the plain of Nakhchivan. Ismail was fourteen. Alvand commanded perhaps thirty thousand men - four or five times Ismail's strength. The Qizilbash charged anyway, their crimson caps visible across the dust, and broke the Aqqoyunlu line. Alvand fled westward toward Diyarbakir, leaving the road to Tabriz open.

Ismail entered Tabriz in the autumn of 1501. Tabriz was the great city of the northwest, a mercantile and artistic capital of some 200,000 people, home to the tiled masterpiece of the Blue Mosque, its streets filled with Turkmen courtiers, Persian administrators, Armenian merchants, and a population overwhelmingly Sunni.

In Tabriz, Ismail made the decision that would define everything after. He declared himself Shah of Iran. And he declared that Twelver Shi'ism - the creed of the Twelve Imams descended from Ali - would be the official religion of his realm. The Friday sermon, the khutba, was to be read in the names of the Twelve Imams. The first three caliphs revered by Sunnis - Abu Bakr, Umar, and Uthman - were to be publicly cursed from the pulpits.

His own advisers reportedly warned him. Tabriz was at least two-thirds Sunni. If he pushed too fast he would face revolt, and revolt would mean massacre. According to the chronicles, Ismail answered that God and the Imams stood beside him; any man who resisted would be cut down. The chronicles also report that some were. A campaign of intimidation, execution, and forced conversion accompanied the proclamation. Shrines of Sunni saints were desecrated, prominent ulama who would not submit were killed, and the cemeteries of rival clerics were reportedly exhumed.

What Ismail had done, at fourteen, was audacious almost to the point of recklessness. He had invented a state. He had also planted a religious boundary that would turn every future border with the Ottomans into a sectarian frontier. From the moment the khutba was altered in the great mosque of Tabriz, the political geography of the Middle East had been rewritten.

Conquering Iran: From Baghdad to Herat

The next decade was an almost unbroken sequence of campaigns. Ismail was not a theorist of empire; he was a horseman, and he conquered as horsemen do - by riding, fighting, wintering, and riding again.

In 1503, the surviving Aqqoyunlu sultan Murad, Alvand's cousin and rival, made his bid at Hamadan in the Zagros foothills. Once again Ismail's Qizilbash were outnumbered. Once again they won. The victory at Hamadan ended the Aqqoyunlu as a political force and opened the Iranian plateau. Isfahan opened its gates. Shiraz followed. By 1504, Ismail controlled Fars, the heartland of classical Persian civilization, and Kerman to the southeast. The ancient provinces that had been ruled for three centuries by Turkmen confederations and local lords were being stitched, for the first time since the Mongol collapse, into a single polity ruled from Tabriz.

Ismail then turned west. In 1507 he rode into Iraq and took Najaf and Karbala, the two holiest cities of Shi'ism - the burial places of the Imam Ali and his martyred son Husayn. For a Shi'ite ruler, possession of these shrines carried a weight no treasury could measure. Ismail visited both tombs, prostrated himself, and ordered extensive restorations. To his followers it was the Mahdi returning to his own. To the Sunni world it was an aggression that could no longer be ignored.

In 1508 he captured Van in eastern Anatolia, probing the Ottoman frontier. In 1509 his army took Baghdad itself, the old Abbasid capital, whose population had lived under Turkmen rule for decades. Here too the public cursing of the first three caliphs was imposed, and here too the chronicles record the execution of Sunni notables and the destruction of a number of Sunni shrines, including, according to some accounts, that of Abu Hanifa, the great jurist whose school was dominant among the Ottomans.

By 1510, Ismail's dominion stretched from the Euphrates to Khorasan's border. Only one serious rival remained in the east: the Uzbek confederation under Muhammad Shaybani Khan, who had driven the Timurid prince Babur from Samarkand and was now pushing south into Iran itself. In the summer of 1510, Ismail force-marched his army across the plateau to Merv, in what is now Turkmenistan. He laid an ambush using an old steppe trick - a feigned retreat - and Shaybani took the bait. The Uzbek khan was killed in the rout. According to the best-known account, Ismail had Shaybani's skull mounted in gold and sent to the Ottoman sultan, Bayezid II, as a warning, and his skin stuffed with straw and paraded.

With Shaybani's death, Khorasan fell. Herat, the glittering Timurid capital whose workshops had produced the finest miniature painting and calligraphy in the Islamic world, welcomed Ismail in 1510. At twenty-three, he ruled an empire that ran from the Tigris in the west to the Amu Darya in the east, from the Caucasus in the north to the Persian Gulf in the south. It was the largest Iranian-ruled state since the Arab conquest nine centuries earlier.

Then came Chaldiran. In August 1514, Sultan Selim I of the Ottomans, alarmed by Shi'ite agitation in Anatolia and by Ismail's sheer momentum, led an enormous army eastward. The two sides met on the plain of Chaldiran, northwest of Lake Urmia. The Ottomans brought something Ismail did not: field artillery and massed Janissary musketry. The Qizilbash, still trusting in cavalry charges and the baraka of their shah, were mowed down. Ismail himself was wounded and narrowly escaped capture; one of his wives fell into Ottoman hands. Tabriz was briefly occupied.

Chaldiran did not destroy the Safavid state - Selim's overstretched army retreated before the winter - but it shattered something inside Ismail. The Mahdi had been defeated. The shah who believed himself invincible had seen his men cut down by Ottoman guns. He would never personally lead an army into battle again.

Divine Kingship and the Cult of the Shah

To his Qizilbash, Ismail was never simply a political ruler. He was murshid-i kamil, the Perfect Spiritual Guide of the Safavid order, a hereditary sanctity passed to him from four generations of shaykhs at Ardabil. Through his mother he was a grandson of Uzun Hasan, tying him to the Aqqoyunlu royal house. Through the Safavid genealogical claim - disputed by modern historians but central to the dynasty's self-presentation - he was a descendant of the Seventh Shi'ite Imam, Musa al-Kazim, and therefore of the Prophet himself.

Onto this already extraordinary pedigree his followers grafted something stranger still. Many Qizilbash clans appear to have believed that Ismail was a direct manifestation of the divine - an incarnation of Ali, or of the Hidden Imam who had disappeared in the ninth century and was expected to return at the end of time. They drank to his health from cups they believed he had sanctified merely by looking at them. They rode into battle shouting his name as a war-cry and as a prayer. When ordered, they reportedly threw themselves unarmored against enemy lines in expectation of miraculous protection.

Ismail did not discourage any of this. At court in Tabriz he dressed in the crimson cap of his father's order but sat on the throne of Persian kings. He adopted the old Iranian title of padishah - great king - while retaining the Sufi title of murshid. It was a fusion no ruler before him had attempted on this scale: the shah as king, saint, and redeemer at once.

The practical consequences were enormous. Because his authority was sacred as well as political, Ismail could impose Twelver Shi'ism on a population that was overwhelmingly Sunni in 1501, and he could do it quickly. He imported Shi'ite scholars from the Arab lands - from Jabal Amil in modern Lebanon, from Bahrain, from Iraq - because Iran itself had too few trained Twelver clerics to staff the new mosques, courts, and madrasas. He endowed shrines. He funded pilgrimages. He built, over two decades, the scaffolding of a religious establishment that would outlast his dynasty and, in a sense, outlast every dynasty that followed.

Historians differ on how sincerely Ismail believed his own divinity. Some read the sources as the words of a young man genuinely convinced he was the instrument of the Imams. Others read them as the calculated theater of a politician who understood that his army's fanaticism was his greatest weapon and must be fed. The truth is probably both. Belief and utility rarely run on separate tracks in the minds of those who wield power.

Chaldiran in 1514 broke the spell but not the structure. The Qizilbash doctrine of the infallible shah would fade, and later Safavid rulers would rely more on the formal authority of the ulama than on mystical charisma. But the religious infrastructure Ismail built would remain. Iran, alone among the great Muslim lands, had become Shi'ite.

The Poetry of Khatai

There is a second Ismail, and he did not wield a sword. He wrote verse. Under the pen name Khatai - meaning "the sinner" or "the errant one," a traditional mark of humility among Sufi poets - Ismail composed a substantial divan in Azeri Turkish, the language of his mother and his army. A smaller body of his work survives in Persian.

The poems are extraordinary for what they reveal. In them Ismail announces, in the first person, exactly what his Qizilbash believed about him:

Lines like these, scattered through Khatai's divan, are not metaphor dressed up for a Sufi audience familiar with such tropes. Read alongside the behavior of the Qizilbash, they look like a theology of kingship stated in verse. The shah is the manifestation of the divine; his followers are his disciples; the boundary between prayer and obedience has been erased.

Yet Khatai also wrote quieter poems - love lyrics in the classical ghazal form, laments for fallen comrades, verses in praise of Ali and the Twelve Imams. He drew on the Turkish folk tradition as well as on the Persian high style of Hafiz and Rumi, and the mixture shaped a new literary idiom. His work became a foundational text for what would later be called Azerbaijani Turkish literature, recited in the coffeehouses and dervish lodges of Anatolia and the Caucasus for centuries.

Khatai's poems mattered strategically as well as culturally. They circulated orally among the Qizilbash tribes of Anatolia, beyond the reach of Ottoman censors, and they kept Safavid loyalty alive in villages the Safavid army could not reach. A poem could be memorized. A poem could cross a border. In the long struggle with the Ottomans, Ismail's verses were a kind of soft power, and the Ottoman sultans knew it. Selim I, himself a fine Persian poet, reportedly kept a copy of Khatai's work and wrote replies to it in verse.

Key Figures & Events

- **Shah Ismail I (1487-1524)**: Founder of the Safavid dynasty, crowned at fourteen, poet under the name Khatai.

- **Shaykh Haydar**: Ismail's father, who militarized the Safavid order and devised the crimson Qizilbash cap; killed in 1488.

- **Karkiya Mirza Ali**: Shi'ite lord of Lahijan who sheltered Ismail during his years in hiding.

- **Muhammad Shaybani Khan**: Uzbek leader killed at Merv in 1510, clearing Khorasan for Safavid rule.

- **Sultan Selim I**: Ottoman ruler who defeated Ismail at Chaldiran in 1514 with artillery and musketry.

- **Capture of Tabriz (1501)**: Beginning of the Safavid state and of Twelver Shi'ism as state religion.

- **Battle of Chaldiran (1514)**: First major Safavid defeat, ending the myth of Ismail's invincibility.

Analysis

In thirteen years, between walking out of Lahijan in 1499 and receiving the submission of Herat in 1510, Ismail accomplished something that should not have been possible. He gathered a network of Anatolian and Azerbaijani tribes into a disciplined army, defeated every major power between the Caucasus and the Oxus, and imposed a minority religion on a vast Sunni population - all before the age at which most modern politicians finish school.

The reasons were structural as much as personal. The Aqqoyunlu had broken into feuding fragments. The Timurids in the east had exhausted themselves. The Ottomans were preoccupied with their own succession and with Europe. Into this vacuum stepped a movement with a ready-made ideology, a motivated soldiery, and a charismatic child at its head. Ismail was the accelerant, not the whole fire.

What lasted was not the conquests themselves - many of those lands would be lost and regained repeatedly over the next two centuries - but the religious settlement. By fusing kingship, Sufism, and Twelver Shi'ism into a single political identity, Ismail created a country that could not easily be absorbed by its Sunni neighbors and could not easily fragment along tribal lines. Chaldiran showed the limits of his military vision. But even after Chaldiran, the Shi'ite state he had declared in the Tabriz mosque in 1501 continued to function. That was the real conquest.

Quick Summary

- Ismail spent his boyhood in hiding in Gilan after his father's death in battle and his brother's killing in 1494.

- He emerged in 1499, avenged his father at Shirvan in 1500-1501, and defeated the Aqqoyunlu at Sharur.

- He took Tabriz in 1501 and declared Twelver Shi'ism the state religion, cursing the first three Sunni caliphs from the pulpits.

- Between 1503 and 1510 he conquered Hamadan, Fars, Kerman, Najaf, Karbala, Van, Baghdad, and Herat.

- His Qizilbash followers regarded him as a divine figure, an incarnation of the Imams or even of God.

- As the poet Khatai he wrote Azeri Turkish verse proclaiming his sacred identity and shaping a new literary tradition.

- The Ottoman victory at Chaldiran in 1514 ended his aura of invincibility; he never led an army again.

- His religious settlement - the Shi'ite identity of Iran - outlasted him and endures today.

Ismail died in 1524, not yet thirty-seven, a man who had spent the last decade of his life in the shadow of a single defeat. He left behind a ten-year-old son, Tahmasp, who would inherit both the empire and the unresolved problems his father had bequeathed: a Qizilbash aristocracy that believed itself divinely authorized to choose its own leaders, an Ottoman neighbor with better artillery, and a population still being converted, mosque by mosque, to the faith its shah had imposed. The crimson crown had been forged. Whether it could be kept on an Iranian head was the question the next century would answer.

The crimson crown had been forged, but forging a kingdom and forging a nation are not the same act. Ismail had welded the plateau together with cavalry and charisma; what he did next would outlast both. Alongside the campaigns that carried him from Tabriz to Baghdad, he launched a second conquest, quieter but more permanent, aimed not at territory but at the souls of its inhabitants. It was this second campaign, pursued from the pulpit and enforced at the sword's point, whose consequences would still be visible five centuries later, long after the battles had blurred into legend.

Chapter 3:

Imposing the Twelver Faith

When Shah Ismail rode into Tabriz in the summer of 1501, perhaps one in ten of its citizens prayed as Shi'a. He announced from the pulpit of the congregational mosque that the rest would convert - or die. Within a century, Iran would stand as the only Twelver Shi'i state on earth.

No single decree in Iranian history has shaped the country so profoundly, or so permanently. The religious revolution Ismail launched at fourteen years old would outlast his dynasty, survive invasions and revolutions, and still define the Islamic Republic five centuries later. Yet it was also one of the most violent religious transformations the medieval world had seen: a program of coerced belief imposed by sword-wielding tribesmen on a population that, for the most part, had never considered itself anything but Sunni. To understand how a frontier Sufi order turned a predominantly Sunni land into the beating heart of global Shi'ism, three things demand close attention - the religious map Ismail inherited, the brutal machinery by which he redrew it, and the quieter, more consequential work of the clerics he later imported to give his revolution intellectual roots.

The Religious Landscape of Late Medieval Iran

The Iran that Ismail conquered was not a religious monolith. It was a patchwork of loyalties, a place where a traveler could cross three valleys in a week and pray behind three different imams in three different traditions.

The great majority of Iranians in 1500 were Sunni, and most followed the Shafi'i or Hanafi legal schools. The cities of Khorasan -

Herat, Nishapur, Mashhad - were celebrated centers of Sunni learning, their madrasas producing jurists whose commentaries were read from Cairo to Delhi. Tabriz, Isfahan, Shiraz: all were overwhelmingly Sunni, though each housed its own minorities, its own local saints, its own peculiar devotional life.

Sunni Islam in Iran, however, was not the austere, legally precise religion one might find in Mamluk Cairo. It was saturated with Sufism. Brotherhoods - the Naqshbandi, the Kubrawi, the Nurbakhshi - organized spiritual life across the region, their lodges serving as hostels, schools, and political clearinghouses. Veneration of holy men, pilgrimages to shrines, devotion to the family of the Prophet: these practices cut across sectarian boundaries. A Sunni in fifteenth-century Kashan might weep for Husayn at Karbala as readily as any Shi'i.

This blurring mattered. It meant that the line between Sunni and Shi'i piety, so sharp in theological treatises, was often invisible on the ground. Love of Ali, reverence for the Twelve Imams, mourning for the martyrs of Karbala - these were common currency among Iranian Muslims regardless of their formal allegiance. The historian Marshall Hodgson called this phenomenon "Alid loyalism," and it was everywhere.

Shi'ism proper existed in scattered but significant pockets. The holy cities of Qom and Sabzavar were Twelver strongholds, as were parts of Mazandaran along the Caspian coast and enclaves in Iraq and Bahrain. Descendants of the Prophet - sayyids - enjoyed status and sometimes political power. Under the Mongol Ilkhans in the thirteenth and fourteenth centuries, Shi'i scholars had briefly flourished at court. But Twelver Shi'ism as a mass phenomenon, as the faith of a whole kingdom, simply did not exist.

Complicating matters further were the *ghulat* - the "exaggerators" - sects whose beliefs stretched far beyond orthodox Twelver theology. They saw Ali as a manifestation of divinity, anticipated a returning messiah, and often mixed Islam with older Anatolian and Turkic traditions. Ismail's own movement, the Safaviyya, had begun as a Sunni Sufi order in the thirteenth century but by his lifetime had drifted into this charged *ghulat* territory. His Turkmen followers, the Qizilbash, believed him to be something close to a god.

Onto this variegated religious map Ismail would now impose a single, enforced orthodoxy. It was an act without precedent in the Islamic world.

The Forced Conversion: Methods and Resistance

The conversion was not a gentle reform. It was a program of terror executed over decades by men who believed, with genuine conviction, that they were purifying the earth.

At Tabriz in 1501, Ismail's advisers reportedly warned him against public proclamation of Shi'ism. The city was Sunni; there would be riots. Ismail, according to the chronicler Khwandamir, drew his sword and declared that God and the Imams stood with him - and that if the people resisted, he would kill every one of them. He then mounted the pulpit and ordered the Friday prayer recited in the Twelver formula, with the names of the Twelve Imams and the ritual cursing of the first three caliphs whom Sunnis revere.

The formula was the key. Sunni Muslims hold Abu Bakr, Umar, and Uthman as righteous successors to the Prophet. For Twelver Shi'is, they were usurpers who cheated Ali of his rightful inheritance. To curse them publicly - the Arabic term is *tabarra* - was not a theological nuance. It was an act of sectarian violence, a line drawn in blood across the Muslim community.

Squads of Qizilbash enforcers, sometimes called *tabarra'iyan*, roamed the streets of conquered cities demanding that ordinary people recite the curse aloud. Those who refused were killed. Those who complied, regardless of their inner beliefs, were counted as converted. In some accounts, the executioners ate the flesh of their victims as a gesture of ritual contempt - a detail that appears in multiple contemporary chronicles and that, even allowing for exaggeration, tells us something about the atmosphere of the early Safavid conquest.

Resistance was considerable and often doomed. In Herat, which Ismail took in 1510, the Sunni scholarly establishment was decimated. Leading ulama were executed or driven into exile. Shrines associated with Sunni saints were vandalized; tombs were desecrated. The tomb of the Sunni theologian Abu Hanifa, in Baghdad, which fell briefly to the Safavids in 1508, was reportedly destroyed. So too was the tomb of the medieval jurist Abd al-Qadir al-Gilani.

Many Sunni scholars simply fled. They went east to the Uzbek lands and Mughal India, or west to Ottoman territory, carrying manuscripts, grievances, and a bitter narrative of Safavid barbarism that would shape Sunni polemics against Shi'ism for centuries. Herat's losses were Samarkand's and Bukhara's gains. Iran's intellectual hemorrhage in these decades was severe.

Popular resistance took subtler forms. In rural Khorasan and in parts of Kurdistan, communities maintained Sunni practice quietly, conforming in public, dissenting in private. Entire districts were only nominally converted; it would take a second and third generation of pressure, under later Safavid shahs, to complete the work Ismail had begun.

Violence was not confined to Sunnis. Jews, Christians, and Zoroastrians faced sporadic persecutions under Safavid rule, sometimes forced to wear distinguishing marks, sometimes pressured to convert, their legal status at the mercy of a shah's mood or a cleric's sermon. The dream of a purified Twelver realm pressed hardest on non-Muslims, but it pressed on everyone.

By the time Ismail died in 1524, broken by his defeat at Chaldiran a decade earlier, the project was irreversible. The infrastructure of Sunni Islam in Iran - its madrasas, its networks, its leading scholars - had been shattered. What remained was a religious vacuum. The question was who would fill it.

Importing Arab Ulama from Jabal Amil and Bahrain

Here lay the great paradox of Ismail's revolution. He had proclaimed Twelver Shi'ism as the state religion of Iran. But Iran had almost no Twelver scholars. Who would teach the people what they were now required to believe?

The shah, and his successors, solved the problem by importing clerics from the one place where Twelver learning had survived and flourished: the Arab lands. Specifically, from two modest regions that would play an outsized role in shaping Iranian religious life - Jabal Amil in what is now southern Lebanon, and the oasis archipelago of Bahrain on the Persian Gulf.

Jabal Amil was a hilly, poor district of villages tucked into the mountains above the Mediterranean. For reasons obscure to historians, it had become, by the fourteenth century, a stronghold of Twelver Shi'i scholarship. Living under Sunni Mamluk and later Ottoman rule, its clerics developed a rigorous jurisprudential tradition in relative isolation. They were learned, disciplined, and - crucially - underemployed, since no Shi'i state existed to patronize them.

The Safavid invitation changed their world. Beginning in the early sixteenth century and accelerating through the seventeenth, Arab ulama packed up their libraries and rode or sailed east to Iran. They were given stipends, endowments, teaching posts, judgeships. Some rose to become the most powerful religious figures in the empire.

The most celebrated was Ali al-Karaki, an Amili scholar who arrived in Ismail's reign and became the chief religious authority under his son Tahmasp. Al-Karaki was granted unprecedented powers: he could appoint prayer leaders, collect religious taxes, issue binding legal rulings. His appointment created a new institution in effect - the office of the state-sponsored Shi'i jurist, the *mujtahid* empowered by royal decree.

This was revolutionary in itself. In classical Twelver theory, the Twelfth Imam was in occultation - hidden, to return at the end of time - and in his absence no temporal government could be fully legitimate. Scholars like al-Karaki began to argue that qualified jurists could act as the Imam's deputies in matters of law, taxation, and even warfare. The seed of the idea that would flower, four centuries later, in Khomeini's doctrine of *velayat-e faqih* - the rule of the jurist - was planted in the Safavid court by a Lebanese cleric.

Bahrain contributed its own dynasty of scholars, the Bahranis, who specialized in hadith and philosophy and who populated the seminaries of Isfahan and Mashhad through the seventeenth century. Yusuf al-Bahrani, though he lived later, epitomized the erudite, rigorous style these Arab emigres brought with them.

The effect on Iranian religious life was profound and lasting. Twelver Shi'ism in Iran was built from above, by Arab specialists operating under royal patronage, imposing standardized texts, standardized rituals, and standardized law on a population learning its new faith. The old Iranian Sufi networks, which had long provided spiritual leadership, were systematically displaced. Shrines were reorganized, seminaries founded, curricula fixed.

By the time of Shah Abbas I, who reigned from 1588 to 1629, Isfahan had become the intellectual capital of world Shi'ism, a role it would hold until the rise of Najaf in Iraq two centuries later. The city's madrasas attracted students from Bahrain, Iraq, India, and beyond. The ulama class had become indispensable to the state - and would, in time, grow strong enough to challenge it.

Ritual Cursing and the Sunni-Shi'a Rupture

Public cursing of the first three caliphs was not a minor liturgical detail. It was a political weapon aimed squarely at the Ottoman Empire, and it tore Sunni and Shi'i Islam apart with an efficiency no theological treatise could match.

Before the Safavids, Sunni and Shi'i Muslims had certainly disagreed, sometimes violently. But they had also lived together across much of the Islamic world, shared shrines, intermarried, prayed side by side at the Hajj. The boundary was porous. Polemicists existed, but so did the countless ordinary Muslims who moved through the blurred middle ground of Alid loyalism.

Tabarra made that middle ground uninhabitable. To curse Abu Bakr and Umar in public was to declare, unambiguously and unbearably, that one rejected the historical foundations of Sunni Islam. The ritual was performed in mosques, in processions, in the Muharram observances that the Safavids expanded and codified. It entered the daily life of ordinary Iranians in a way that more abstract theological differences never could.

Ottoman sultans responded in kind. The Ottoman mufti Ebussuud issued fatwas declaring the Qizilbash apostates whose blood could be lawfully shed. Selim I, before his victory at Chaldiran in 1514, is said to have massacred some forty thousand suspected Safavid sympathizers in Anatolia. Ottoman polemics increasingly portrayed Shi'ism not as a Muslim sect in error but as a heresy beyond the pale of Islam. Shi'i polemics returned the compliment.

A hard border, religious as well as political, was forming across the Middle East. A Muslim in sixteenth-century Baghdad now had to choose a side in a way his grandfather had not. The porous cosmopolitan Islam of the medieval world was giving way to something more modern, more binary, and more dangerous - confessional states, each defining itself against the heresy of its neighbor.

The consequences would echo for centuries. The sectarian geography of the modern Middle East - Shi'i Iran, Sunni Turkey, the bitter contest between them for influence over Iraq, Syria, Lebanon, the Gulf - was mapped out in those early sixteenth-century decades, in the cursing formulas of Safavid preachers and the killing fatwas of Ottoman muftis. It is a map that has not finished being redrawn.

The Long Shadow: Why Iran Is Shi'i Today

Forced conversions are common in history. Lasting ones are rare. The Spanish expulsion of the Jews and the Moriscos, the Christianization of pagan Europe, the Islamization of Central Asia - these were slow, partial, contested processes. Why did the Safavid project succeed so completely?

Several answers suggest themselves. The violence was severe and sustained, but violence alone does not explain it: plenty of coerced converts revert when coercion ends. The Safavid dynasty lasted more than two centuries, long enough for three or four generations to grow up knowing nothing else. A child born in Isfahan in 1550 heard her grandchildren's first prayers in 1620, and by then the religion of the state was simply the religion of the family.

The imported Arab ulama built institutions that outlasted the dynasty that patronized them. The seminaries, the legal courts, the network of mosques and shrines, the standardized rituals of Muharram and Ashura - all took root so deeply that the fall of the Safavids in 1736 barely disturbed them. When Nadir Shah tried briefly to reconcile Iran with Sunni Islam in the mid-eighteenth century, he failed utterly. The ulama resisted; the people had moved on.

Shi'ism also fused, over time, with Iranian national identity. The Safavid-Ottoman conflict made Sunni Islam feel foreign, the religion of the Turkish enemy. Persian literature, poetry, art, and architecture absorbed Shi'i themes and became inseparable from them. To be Iranian was to mourn for Husayn, to visit the shrine at Mashhad, to await the Twelfth Imam's return. A religious identity imposed by conquest became, within a few generations, a source of pride and cohesion.

The doctrine itself evolved to fit its new home. The Arab jurists' elevation of the *mujtahid* as deputy of the Hidden Imam gave Iranian Shi'ism an organizational structure that Sunni Islam lacked - a clerical hierarchy capable of mobilizing the faithful, administering law, and, when the moment came, overthrowing a shah. The 1979 revolution was a late, strange fruit of the tree Ismail planted in Tabriz in 1501.

Quick Summary

- In 1501, Shah Ismail proclaimed Twelver Shi'ism the state religion of an Iran whose population was roughly 90 percent Sunni.

- Conversion was enforced by Qizilbash squads through public ritual cursing of the first three caliphs, backed by the sword.

- Sunni scholars were killed or driven into exile in Ottoman lands, Uzbek Central Asia, and Mughal India; shrines were destroyed.

- To fill the clerical vacuum, the Safavids imported Arab Twelver ulama from Jabal Amil in Lebanon and from Bahrain.

- Ali al-Karaki and his successors built a state-sponsored clerical establishment that centralized and standardized Iranian Shi'ism.

- The ritual of *tabarra* hardened the Sunni-Shi'i divide into a lasting sectarian border, mirrored by Ottoman counter-measures.

- Over several generations, Shi'ism fused with Iranian national identity and survived the fall of the Safavid dynasty itself.

Ismail's religious revolution is the Safavid legacy that has outlived all others. The empire he founded is gone; its borders have been redrawn a dozen times; its court culture survives mainly in museums. But the faith he forced onto Iran at sword's point in 1501 still defines the country today. It shapes its politics, its alliances, its enemies, its self-understanding. Few acts of state violence have proved so enduring, and few have more thoroughly demonstrated that a nation's soul, once remade, is very difficult to restore.

A nation's soul, once remade, is very difficult to restore - but the man who remade Iran's soul was not, it turned out, invulnerable. The religious revolution Ismail imposed rested on a claim about his own person: that he was more than a king, that God spoke through him, that his warriors rode into battle accompanied by the unseen hosts of the Twelve Imams. Such a claim could survive almost anything except a clear, public, military refutation. In the summer of 1514, on a dusty plain called Chaldiran, an Ottoman sultan arrived with cannon and quiet contempt, prepared to deliver exactly that.

Chapter 4:

Chaldiran and the Ottoman Wound

For thirteen years Shah Ismail had been untouchable. He had ridden out of Gilan as a fourteen-year-old fugitive, crushed rival after rival, and convinced his Qizilbash warriors that he was not merely a king but a living manifestation of the divine. Then, on a dusty plain in eastern Anatolia, an Ottoman sultan with a column of cannons and a quiet contempt for miracles proved otherwise.

The Battle of Chaldiran, fought on August 23, 1514, is one of those engagements whose consequences outran the day itself. In a single afternoon it halted Safavid expansion into Anatolia, drew a rough border between Sunni and Shia empires that still haunts the map of the Middle East, and broke something inside Ismail himself. He would live another decade, but he never again led an army into battle, and he is said never again to have smiled with the old abandon. The wound at Chaldiran was geographic, political, and deeply personal. To understand how Iran became what it is, and how the Ottomans became the power they were, we have to stand on that plain with the gunners and the horsemen and watch the smoke rise.

Selim the Grim and the Ottoman Threat

Sultan Selim I came to the Ottoman throne in 1512 by the simple expedient of deposing his father and having his brothers strangled. His enemies called him Yavuz - meaning stern, severe, or grim. He earned the name. Where his father Bayezid II had preferred piety and poetry, Selim preferred campaigns and corpses. He was a soldier first and a ruler second, and he looked eastward with a cold clarity his father had lacked.

What Selim saw in Safavid Iran alarmed him. Ismail's preachers, the khalifas, were crossing into Anatolia and finding eager audiences among the Turkmen tribes of the eastern provinces. These were the same tribes from which the Ottoman army drew much of its traditional strength, and their loyalty was drifting. In 1511, a Qizilbash uprising in central Anatolia led by a charismatic rebel called Shahkulu had come close to destabilizing the entire region. For the Ottomans, the Safavid threat was not merely a rival empire on a distant frontier. It was a fifth column operating inside Ottoman borders, a theological insurgency that promised to hollow out the sultanate from within.

Selim responded with the brutal thoroughness that became his signature. By some accounts, he ordered the registration of Shia sympathizers in eastern Anatolia and had tens of thousands killed or deported. The exact figures are disputed, and later chroniclers may have inflated them, but the policy itself is not in doubt. Selim was determined to cauterize the wound before marching east to find its source.

He also sought religious cover. Ottoman jurists produced fatwas declaring the Qizilbash heretics, and war against them not merely permissible but obligatory. Selim sent Ismail a series of letters, preserved in Ottoman archives, whose tone shifted from mocking to openly contemptuous. He addressed the Shah as a mere dervish, a charlatan dressed up as a king. Ismail replied with the language of sovereign equality and, according to one tradition, sent back a box of opium, implying that his rival must be intoxicated to write such nonsense.

By the spring of 1514, Selim had assembled an army of roughly sixty thousand men at Edirne and was marching east. His supply lines were long, his janissaries were grumbling about the distance, and summer in the Anatolian plateau was merciless. But Selim had something Ismail did not: a core of disciplined infantry armed with matchlock muskets, and a park of field artillery that could be lashed together into a wall of iron.

He was not marching merely to punish a rival. He was marching to prove that an idea, however charismatic, could be killed by gunpowder.

Gunpowder Versus Cavalry: A Technological Mismatch

To appreciate what happened at Chaldiran, one has to understand the two different theories of war that collided there. Ismail's army was built around the Qizilbash, the red-capped Turkmen tribal cavalry whose devotion to the Shah was religious in the literal sense. They believed he could not be defeated. They believed their arrows, guided by his baraka, would find Ottoman hearts without effort. They fought in the classic steppe tradition: fast, ferocious, reliant on the shock of the charge and the skill of the horse archer.

This was not an outdated approach. It had conquered Iran, cowed Central Asia, and shattered the Aq Qoyunlu. Against other cavalry armies, the Qizilbash were formidable. The problem was that they were about to meet something else.

The Ottoman army that Selim led across Anatolia represented a decades-long experiment in integrating gunpowder into the traditional structures of Islamic warfare. At its heart stood the janissaries, a standing infantry corps recruited through the devshirme levy of Christian boys, converted to Islam, drilled relentlessly, and increasingly armed with matchlock firearms. Around them were the sipahi cavalry, a more conventional force. And decisively, the Ottomans deployed field artillery in numbers unmatched in the region: hundreds of cannons of varying calibers, many cast under European supervision or by European renegades serving Ottoman paymasters.

What made the Ottoman system genuinely new was tactical. At Chaldiran, the Ottomans employed a formation the Europeans would later call the wagon fort - tabur cengi in Turkish, borrowed in part from Hungarian practice. Wagons and gun carriages were chained together in a long line, creating an improvised fortress in the middle of an open plain. Behind this wall the janissaries leveled their muskets. In front of it the cannons were laid. Cavalry charging such a position would meet a killing zone that horses and courage alone could not cross.

Ismail had no equivalent. The Safavids possessed some firearms, but they regarded them with a certain cultural disdain. Muskets were heavy, slow to load, and, in the aristocratic cavalry ethos of the Qizilbash, slightly shameful. A warrior did not blast his enemy from a distance like a merchant defending a warehouse; he rode him down, eye to eye. There are reports that Ismail was offered the chance to attack the Ottomans during their long, vulnerable march, when their guns were still on the road and their troops exhausted. He refused. Chivalric honor forbade ambushing a tired enemy.

In strictly military terms, this decision may have been the single costliest act of Ismail's reign. It allowed Selim to reach Chaldiran, deploy his cannons, chain his wagons, and wait. By the time the two armies faced each other, the question was no longer whether Qizilbash courage could overcome Ottoman numbers. The question was whether flesh could overcome iron. The answer, on most battlefields of the sixteenth century, was no, and it was increasingly so in the decades to come. At Chaldiran, the future of warfare was being rehearsed, and the Safavids had cast themselves in the role of the past.

The Battle of Chaldiran, August 23, 1514

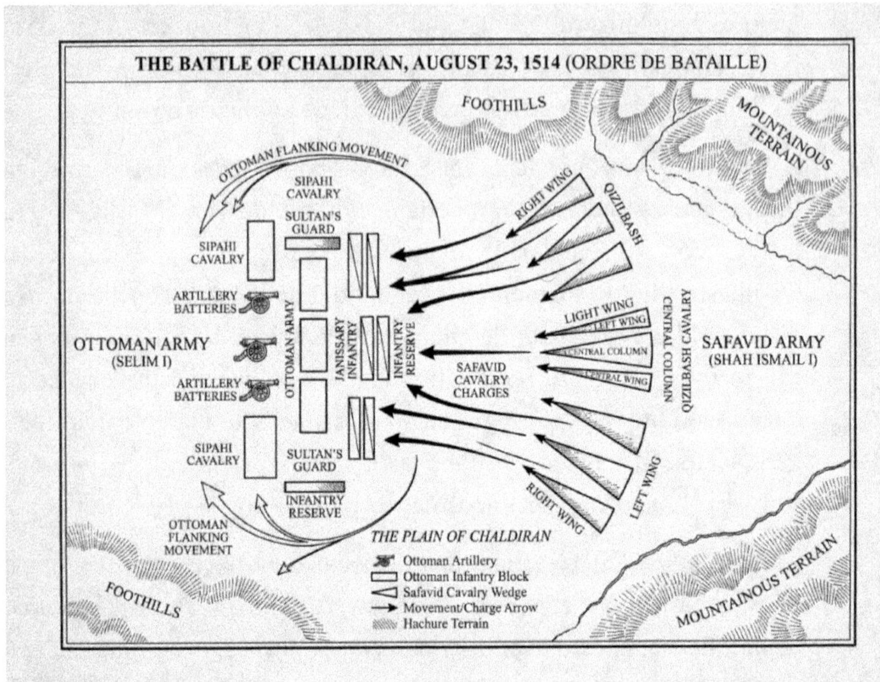

Chaldiran: Order of Battle, August 23, 1514

The plain of Chaldiran lies in what is now the far northwest of Iran, just east of Lake Van - a dry expanse ringed by low hills. On the morning of August 23, 1514, the sky was clear, the ground hard, and the air already hot. Ismail had perhaps forty thousand men, a mix of Qizilbash cavalry and allied contingents. Selim had around sixty thousand, and perhaps two hundred cannons.

Accounts of the battle vary in detail, but the broad sequence is agreed. The Ottomans anchored their center on the wagon fort, cannons forward, janissaries behind, and arrayed their cavalry on the wings. Ismail, displaying the tactical instincts of a cavalry commander rather than a general of combined arms, divided his force into two wings and prepared to envelop the Ottoman flanks, leaving the fortified center to fend for itself.

The initial Safavid charge went well. The Qizilbash right, led by Ismail himself, smashed into the Ottoman left wing and drove it back in disorder. On the other flank, commanded by the veteran Mohammad Khan Ustajlu, the Safavids also made headway. For perhaps an hour it seemed that the old magic was holding, that cavalry elan could still decide a battle by the force of its first impact.

Then the flanks closed in on the Ottoman center, and the center spoke.

Cannons opened fire at close range, followed by volleys from the janissary muskets. Horses screamed and fell. Riders were cut apart by grapeshot at distances at which they could not even close with their enemies. Ustajlu was killed. Whole units of Qizilbash, charging forward in tight formation, disintegrated into chaos. The smoke was so thick, one chronicler wrote, that men fought by the sound of each other's voices.

Ismail himself led charge after charge, personally fighting hand to hand. A mace blow left him wounded; his horse was shot from under him; at one point he was nearly captured and was saved only by a loyal retainer who cried out that he was the Shah, drawing pursuit onto himself so that Ismail could escape. By late afternoon the Safavid army had ceased to exist as a coherent force. Survivors streamed east, leaving their dead, their wounded, their baggage, and, famously, several of Ismail's wives in Ottoman hands.

Estimates of casualties are uncertain. The Safavids may have lost five thousand dead on the field, perhaps far more when stragglers were counted; the Ottomans perhaps two thousand. Numbers, though, understate what had happened. What died at Chaldiran was not primarily a quantity of soldiers. It was an idea.

The Qizilbash had believed that Ismail could not be defeated because he was more than a man. They had ridden into battle convinced that arrows would part around him, that Ottoman cannons would misfire, that the universe itself took sides. They had watched their comrades torn apart by grapeshot while their Shah bled into the dust. Something essential in the relationship between ruler and follower cracked that afternoon, and the crack never fully healed. For the rest of the Safavid century, the Qizilbash would remain a powerful force, but they would also remain a faction-ridden, mistrustful one, and no later Safavid monarch could command them with the divine certainty Ismail had once possessed.

Selim stood on the battlefield, surveyed the dead, and ordered the pursuit. The road to Tabriz was open.

The Sack of Tabriz and Its Consequences

Tabriz, the Safavid capital, lay roughly a week's march to the east. Selim entered the city in early September 1514. There was no resistance; Ismail had fled further east, into the Iranian interior, and the population could only hope for mercy.

Mercy was mixed. Selim did not put Tabriz to the torch, perhaps because he still nursed ambitions of holding it. He prayed in the great congregational mosque, received the submission of the notables, and had the Friday sermon - the khutba - delivered in his own name, the supreme gesture of sovereignty in the Islamic world. For a few weeks in the autumn of 1514, Tabriz was an Ottoman city.

Selim also engaged in a quieter, more lasting form of plunder. He ordered a systematic deportation of Tabriz's craftsmen, scholars, and artists to Istanbul. Several hundred families of weavers, miniaturists, goldsmiths, and architects were marched west, along with the contents of workshops and libraries. Tabriz had been one of the great centers of Persian artistic culture under the Aq Qoyunlu; now its treasures and its makers were absorbed into the Ottoman capital, where they would help shape the distinctive Ottoman style of the classical age. The famous tile work of Iznik, the refinement of Ottoman manuscript painting, the architectural confidence of Sinan's generation - all owe something to the talent extracted from Tabriz in the aftermath of Chaldiran.

Selim's hold on the city proved brief. His janissaries, as was their habit, began to grumble about the distance from home, the approaching winter, and the absence of further plunder. Facing a potential mutiny, Selim withdrew westward within weeks of his arrival. Ismail crept back to find his capital damaged but not destroyed, its people shaken, its workshops hollowed out.

The strategic consequences were more durable than the occupation itself. Selim annexed a long arc of territory along what became the frontier: much of eastern Anatolia, the Kurdish principalities around Diyarbakir, and, within a few years, the Arab lands of Syria, Egypt, and the Hejaz, whose conquest in 1516 and 1517 would make Selim the custodian of Mecca and Medina and, by extension, the leading Sunni sovereign of the age. Chaldiran did not only wound the Safavids; it launched the Ottomans into their imperial maturity.

The border that took shape after Chaldiran would prove remarkably stable. With modifications, it is roughly the border that today separates Turkey from Iran. A line drawn in blood and gunpowder in 1514 remains visible on every modern map of the region - a reminder that some battles do not merely decide wars, they decide geographies.

Ismail's Final Decade: Silence and Decline

The man who returned to Tabriz in the late autumn of 1514 was not the man who had ridden out of it. Ismail was twenty-seven years old. He had another decade to live. He would spend it in a kind of political half-life, drinking heavily, retreating from campaigns, and leaving the business of empire to his officials.

Contemporaries noticed the change immediately. The Venetian ambassadors who had once described Ismail as radiant and beloved now recorded reports of a melancholy ruler given to long silences and heavy wine. He wore black after Chaldiran, it was said, and had black banners carried before him. He ordered no new military adventures against the Ottomans. When his frontier generals pressed him for reinforcements, his responses were slow and ambivalent. The restless prophet-king had become a haunted administrator.

His religious persona also quieted. The wild, apocalyptic poetry of his youth, composed under the pen name Khatai, continued to circulate, but Ismail himself appears to have stopped producing the ecstatic claims that had once thrilled his followers. He had, after all, been proved mortal in the most public way possible. The theological architecture of his movement had taken a hit from which it never fully recovered, and Ismail appears to have understood this. He became, in effect, a more conventional Muslim sovereign - Shia, certainly, but no longer a living messiah.

His empire did not collapse. Safavid administrators, many of them Persian bureaucrats inherited from earlier dynasties, kept the machinery running. Tax collectors collected, governors governed, the qazis adjudicated. Ismail's name remained on the coinage and in the Friday prayer. But real power drifted toward court factions, and the Qizilbash tribes, no longer held in check by the Shah's charisma, began the process of internal feuding that would paralyze Safavid politics for the next generation.

Ismail died in May 1524, probably of a disease aggravated by long alcoholism. He was not yet thirty-seven. He left a ten-year-old son, Tahmasp, to inherit an empire whose boundaries he had defined but whose confidence he had, in a single August afternoon, quietly surrendered.

Analysis

It is tempting to read Chaldiran as a simple morality tale about technology: the side with the better weapons won. That reading is not wrong, but it is not sufficient. The Ottomans had cannons because they had built, over a century, the administrative and fiscal structures to pay for them, the industrial capacity to cast them, the drilled infantry to protect them, and the intellectual openness to borrow from European practice. The Safavids had not built those structures yet. Ismail's empire was a vehicle of charisma, not a machine of iron.

The deeper lesson of Chaldiran is that charismatic states are fragile in a way bureaucratic states are not. A sultan can lose a battle; a messiah cannot. When Selim's gunners broke the Qizilbash line, they broke the founding premise of the Safavid project. Ismail's heirs would spend the rest of the dynasty trying to rebuild legitimacy on other foundations - on orthodox Shia clerisy, on Persian administrative tradition, on dynastic longevity - precisely because the original foundation had proved too brittle to bear the weight of defeat.

Chaldiran also locked the Safavid and Ottoman empires into a rivalry that would shape the Islamic world for two centuries. Shia Iran and Sunni Turkey became mirror images, defined against each other, each reinforcing its own orthodoxy in opposition to the other. Sectarian boundaries that had been fluid for a thousand years hardened into state ideologies. The modern sectarian geography of the Middle East has many parents, but Selim and Ismail are certainly among them.

Key Figures & Events

- **Sultan Selim I** (1470-1520): Ottoman sultan whose eastern campaign and victory at Chaldiran redefined the Islamic world's balance of power.

- **Shah Ismail I** (1487-1524): Safavid founder whose defeat ended his active military career and broke the myth of his invincibility.

- **Mohammad Khan Ustajlu**: Senior Qizilbash commander killed leading the Safavid left wing at Chaldiran.

- **The Tabur Cengi**: The Ottoman wagon-fort tactic that neutralized Safavid cavalry.

- **Sack and Occupation of Tabriz** (September 1514): Brief Ottoman control of the Safavid capital and the deportation of its artisans to Istanbul.

Quick Summary

- On August 23, 1514, Ottoman forces under Selim I crushed Shah Ismail's Safavid army at Chaldiran in eastern Anatolia.

- The battle pitted Qizilbash cavalry, reliant on religious charisma and shock tactics, against Ottoman cannons, muskets, and disciplined janissaries.

- Selim's use of chained wagons and field artillery created a killing zone that traditional cavalry could not overcome.

- Ismail was wounded, narrowly escaped capture, and saw the Qizilbash belief in his divine invulnerability shattered.

- Selim briefly occupied Tabriz, deporting hundreds of artisans and scholars to Istanbul, enriching Ottoman culture at Safavid expense.

- The defeat halted Safavid westward expansion and fixed an Ottoman-Iranian border that roughly survives today.

- Ismail withdrew from public life, drank heavily, and died in 1524 without leading another campaign.

- Chaldiran hardened the Sunni-Shia divide into a rivalry between two major states that would shape the region for centuries.

The young prophet-king who had ridden out of Gilan to conquer an empire never truly rode again. Ismail would live on for another decade, but the Shah who had spoken as though God spoke through him fell silent after Chaldiran, and the silence had consequences. His son Tahmasp would inherit not only a kingdom but a question: on what foundation could a Safavid state stand now that its founding miracle had been disproved by Ottoman gunpowder? The answer would take a generation to work out, and it would transform Iran in ways Ismail, brooding over his wine in the darkened halls of Tabriz, could not have foreseen.

Ismail fell silent after Chaldiran, and the silence lasted the rest of his life. When he died in 1524, what he left behind was not a settled inheritance but a question: on what foundation could a Safavid state stand now that its founding miracle had been disproved by gunpowder? The answer would have to be worked out not by the prophet-king but by the ten-year-old boy on whose head the crown now rested. It would take fifty-two years, and it would require an entirely different kind of rule - patient where Ismail had been ecstatic, cautious where Ismail had been convinced.

Chapter 5:

Tahmasp and the Long Survival

He was ten years old when they put the crown on his head. His father had been a prophet-king who rode into battle convinced of his own divinity; the boy who inherited the throne would spend the next half-century learning a quieter art - the art of staying alive.

Tahmasp I is the forgotten Safavid. Sandwiched in popular memory between his father Ismail, the charismatic founder, and his great-grandson Abbas, the master-builder, he has often been dismissed as pious, anxious, even reclusive. Yet when he died in 1576, fifty-two years after his accession, he handed on an empire still intact - its borders defended, its doctrine secured, its apparatus of state measurably stronger than the one he had inherited. No other Safavid ruler reigned so long. None faced a grimmer opening hand: civil war among his own guardians, Uzbek raiders on the eastern horizon, and Suleiman the Magnificent, the most powerful monarch in the world, preparing to ride through the western passes. That Iran survived these decades at all is the central fact of the sixteenth century. That it survived them as a recognizable state, with a Shi'a identity hardening into permanence, is Tahmasp's achievement.

A Boy King and the Qizilbash Civil Wars

When Ismail died in May 1524, the Safavid experiment was barely twenty-three years old. The Qizilbash - the Turkmen tribal confederation whose red-capped cavalry had put Ismail on the throne - were the real power behind the crown. They had followed Ismail as a messianic figure. They owed no such devotion to a child.

The boy inherited a court stacked with rival chieftains, each commanding his own troops, each convinced that whoever controlled the young shah controlled Iran. What followed was not a single civil war but a cascade of them. The Ustajlu, Shamlu, Rumlu, Takkalu, and Dhu'l-Qadar tribes turned on one another in a lethal game of musical chairs around Tahmasp's person. Regents rose and fell. One faction's vizier would be murdered by the next. Entire provincial armies marched on the capital to tip the balance.

For nearly a decade, the shah was a hostage of his own guardians. Tabriz, the capital, watched strongmen come and go. In some years Tahmasp was a spectator at his own court; in others, a pawn being moved between the tents of warlords who claimed to protect him.

And yet he was also learning. The boy who watched his regents butcher each other developed an abiding distrust of the Qizilbash that would shape the rest of his reign and, indirectly, the rest of Safavid history. If his father had ruled as the beloved pir of a military brotherhood, Tahmasp would rule as a sovereign above the tribes, or he would not rule at all.

The first sign that the boy might survive came on the battlefield. In 1528, aged fourteen, Tahmasp faced the Uzbek khan Ubayd Allah at Jam, in Khurasan. The Uzbeks had been raiding Safavid territory almost annually since Ismail's death, picking off frontier cities, sacking shrines, dragging off captives. At Jam, Tahmasp used his small complement of Ottoman-style firearms and field artillery to devastating effect. The Uzbek cavalry, lacking gunpowder weapons of comparable quality, broke. The victory did not end the Uzbek threat, which would return in wave after wave through the century, but it established something more important. The boy king could win.

By 1532, after a last round of factional bloodletting, Tahmasp emerged from the chrysalis of his minority as a genuine monarch. He was eighteen. He had seen his guardians poison one another, his tutors beheaded, his empire shrink and bulge with the fortunes of tribal war.

He would spend the rest of his life ensuring no one ever again held him hostage. Slowly, patiently, he began building an alternative power base within his household - drawing increasingly on enslaved Circassians, Georgians, and Armenians captured in Caucasus campaigns. These *ghulams*, loyal to the shah alone, would in time grow into a counterweight to the Qizilbash and, under later rulers, replace them outright. The transformation took generations. Tahmasp laid the first bricks.

The Capital Moves to Qazvin

In 1548, or thereabouts - chroniclers differ on the exact year - Tahmasp made a decision that would have struck his father as bewildering. He abandoned Tabriz.

Tabriz was the beating heart of Safavid power. It was the city where Ismail had been crowned in 1501, the seat of the great bazaar, the home of the Qizilbash tribes' ancestral estates, the symbol of everything the dynasty had fought for. It was also, fatally, less than two hundred miles from the Ottoman frontier.

Suleiman's armies had taken Tabriz three times already. Each occupation was brief - the Ottomans could not supply a force so far from Anatolia through an Iranian winter - but each was humiliating. The capital had been looted, its population terrorized, its treasuries stripped. A state could not function if its seat of government was a forward trench.

Qazvin, by contrast, sat safely in the interior, on the road between the Caspian provinces and central Iran, far enough from the frontier that no Ottoman army could reach it in a single campaigning season. It had good water, a defensible position, and a central location that allowed the shah to respond to threats from either east or west. It lacked Tabriz's romance. That was, in a sense, the point.

The move was more than logistics. It marked a shift in how the Safavids imagined their empire. Ismail had ruled a frontier state, its capital pressed against its enemies like a fist. Tahmasp began to rule an inner empire, withdrawn from its borders, radiating power outward rather than projecting it forward. Court ceremony became more elaborate, access to the shah more restricted. The boy who had been passed between Qizilbash tents now received ambassadors in painted pavilions, seated on a raised dais, speaking through intermediaries.

Qazvin also became a cultural hub. Tahmasp had spent his youth as an accomplished painter and patron - the great *Shahnameh* produced in his atelier, a book of over seven hundred miniatures, stands among the supreme achievements of Persian manuscript art. In Qazvin, his workshops continued to refine a visual vocabulary that would define Iranian taste for centuries. The city would remain the Safavid capital until Abbas moved it to Isfahan a half-century later, and for most of the sixteenth century it was the place where Iranian statecraft was rethought from the ground up.

The Peace of Amasya and Coexistence with the Ottomans

Suleiman the Magnificent ruled for forty-six years, and for more than twenty of them he was, intermittently, at war with Iran. The conflict was not merely territorial. It was confessional, ideological, dynastic. Suleiman claimed leadership of the Sunni world. Tahmasp embodied the Shi'a challenge to that leadership. As long as both states insisted on universal religious claims, their border could never be more than a temporary truce line.

The Ottoman campaigns of 1533-35, 1548-49, and 1553-55 followed a grimly predictable pattern. Suleiman's immense armies - sometimes 100,000 strong, equipped with the finest artillery in the world - would grind eastward across Anatolia, capture Tabriz, march into the Iranian plateau, and then find nothing to fight. Tahmasp had no intention of meeting such a force in open battle. He refused to be drawn.

Instead he practiced what later strategists would call scorched earth. As the Ottomans advanced, Safavid forces drove livestock into the mountains, burned crops, poisoned wells, destroyed mills. The invading army would occupy empty cities and starving countryside. Disease would thin its ranks. Winter would close the passes. Suleiman would withdraw, having taken territory he could not hold. The following spring, Safavid cavalry would drift back and the frontier would return to something like its previous shape.

It was a war of exhaustion, and it exhausted both sides. Ottoman soldiers resented the ruinous marches. The Safavid treasury, already strained by internal rebellion, could barely fund the defense. Iran's western provinces - Azerbaijan, Kurdistan, the Armenian highlands - were hollowed out by two decades of raid and counter-raid. By the early 1550s, even Suleiman, who had every material reason to keep fighting, had begun to see the limits of his own strategy.

A breakthrough came in 1555 at Amasya, a town in northern Anatolia where Suleiman kept a summer palace. Safavid envoys arrived with proposals. Suleiman, perhaps surprised to be negotiating rather than dictating, agreed to terms. The Peace of Amasya was the first formal treaty ever signed between the Ottoman and Safavid empires.

Its terms were a compromise neither side would have accepted a decade earlier. Iran retained Azerbaijan, including Tabriz, along with most of the Caucasus regions of Shirvan and Daghestan. The Ottomans kept Iraq - including Baghdad, which they had taken in 1534, and the Shi'a shrine cities of Najaf and Karbala, a painful loss for Tahmasp. Eastern Anatolia was demarcated, broadly, along the lines that still run today. Both sides agreed to respect each other's borders and cease hostile propaganda.

The treaty held for more than thirty years. By sixteenth-century standards, this was an astonishing peace. It allowed Iran to breathe. Trade routes reopened. Pilgrims could once again travel to the shrines

- Tahmasp even negotiated Safavid access to Najaf and Karbala as a condition of the agreement. Taxes could be collected without the annual fear of invasion. The population began to recover.

Historians have sometimes read Amasya as a Safavid defeat, noting the loss of Baghdad and Iraq. This misreads the strategic picture. The empire Ismail had proclaimed in 1501 could not have survived another twenty years of Ottoman campaigns. Amasya bought time - the rarest and most valuable commodity in sixteenth-century politics - and Tahmasp used it to consolidate everything his father had left unfinished.

Sheltering Humayun: The Mughal Connection

In the summer of 1544, a strange caravan arrived at Tahmasp's court. Its leader was a man in his late thirties, accompanied by perhaps forty exhausted companions and servants. He wore the battered finery of a king and had nothing else. He was Humayun, son of Babur, second emperor of the Mughals - and, for the moment, emperor of nothing at all.

Humayun had been driven out of India by the Afghan rebel Sher Shah Suri. He had lost battles, allies, provinces, brothers. His infant son Akbar had been left behind in Kandahar in the hands of a hostile uncle. He had crossed Sistan in the depths of winter, nearly dying of cold, and arrived in Safavid territory as a royal refugee begging for help.

Tahmasp received him with elaborate hospitality. Persian chroniclers describe a procession of honors - a silk-draped tent, cooks and musicians, a daily allowance of gold. But the shah's kindness came with conditions. Humayun was politely pressed to adopt Shi'a Islam, at least outwardly, and to accept Safavid suzerainty over any territory he might reconquer. Humayun, desperate, agreed. Whether his conversion was sincere or merely diplomatic is a question the sources leave open; Mughal historians later played it down, Safavid ones played it up.

More substantively, Tahmasp provided what Humayun needed most: an army. Twelve thousand Safavid cavalry, under the command of a royal prince, rode east with the exile in 1545. With their help, Humayun retook Kandahar, then Kabul. Over the next decade, he rebuilt his forces and, in 1555, recrossed the Indus to reclaim Delhi. He died the following year, falling down the stairs of his library, but his son Akbar - the greatest of the Mughal emperors - inherited a restored throne.

The Safavid-Mughal relationship never again reached such intimacy. Under Akbar and his successors, the two empires quarreled over Kandahar, the great caravan city that controlled the routes between Iran and India. Possession of Kandahar would ping-pong between them for more than a century. Yet a pattern had been set. The Mughal court absorbed Persian poetry, Persian administration, Persian architectural idioms. Persian became the language of Mughal high culture, spoken at Delhi and Agra as naturally as at Qazvin. Safavid painters and calligraphers migrated east in search of Mughal patronage. An entire cultural ecosystem - what scholars now call the Persianate world - thickened across the subcontinent.

Tahmasp's sheltering of Humayun was, in immediate terms, a shrewd move against a rival Sunni power - Sher Shah's successors in India threatened Safavid interests in Central Asia. In longer perspective, it seeded a civilizational link that outlasted both dynasties. The Persianate influence on Indian culture, still audible in Urdu poetry and visible in Mughal architecture, descends in part from that winter procession of refugees arriving at Tahmasp's gates.

Royal Repentance and the Turn to Sober Piety

Somewhere around 1533, in what chroniclers would later call his Sincere Repentance, Tahmasp banned wine, gambling, hashish, and several varieties of public entertainment across his domains. He ordered taverns closed, musical instruments confiscated, the decorated wine cups of the court melted down. He renounced, in a public edict, the pleasures of his own youth and called upon his subjects to do the same.

This was not a cynical policy. Tahmasp was, by every surviving account, genuinely devout. He dreamed of the Imams and recorded his visions. He performed nightly prayers with ostentatious regularity. He cultivated Shi'a scholars, invited them to court, endowed madrasas, and pressed the ulama to codify the rituals and jurisprudence of the still-young state religion. Where Ismail had embodied Shi'ism as a mystical, almost heretical force, Tahmasp began to normalize it - to transform ecstatic messianism into a sober, legalistic, clerical tradition.

Shi'a scholars from Jabal Amil in Lebanon, invited by Tahmasp and his successors, arrived to fill gaps in Iranian religious knowledge. Their descendants would become pillars of the clerical establishment. Mosques and shrines were renovated. The shah's own patronage of the great shrine at Mashhad, holding the tomb of the eighth Imam, made pilgrimage to it a central rite of Safavid piety. What had been a political identity imposed from above began to sink roots as lived faith.

The royal image shifted accordingly. Tahmasp withdrew from public spectacle. Foreign ambassadors complained of his reclusiveness - the Venetian Michele Membre, who visited the court in the 1530s, found a shah who was accessible enough, but later visitors met a more remote figure. He prayed more, rode less. He stopped, in his last years, even painting, though he had been among the finest royal artists Iran ever produced.

Critics have found this turn sanctimonious. The shah who banned wine was the same shah who, in 1568, ordered the execution of several thousand prisoners after a provincial revolt. Piety and cruelty coexisted at his court as they did at every sixteenth-century court. Yet the religious transformation was real, and it mattered. By the time Tahmasp died in 1576, Iranian Shi'ism had an institutional backbone that had not existed when he inherited the throne.

His death in Qazvin, after a long illness, set off a succession crisis of ferocious intensity. He had never clearly designated an heir. His favorite son Haydar Mirza was killed within hours of the shah's death by supporters of his half-brother Ismail Mirza, who had been imprisoned in a fortress for nearly twenty years. The shah's formidable daughter Pari Khan Khanum helped orchestrate Ismail's release and accession. The new reign would prove short and disastrous. But that is another chapter.

Key Figures & Events

Tahmasp I ruled from 1524 to 1576, the longest reign in Safavid history. Suleiman the Magnificent led three major campaigns against him before accepting peace at Amasya in 1555. Humayun, the exiled Mughal emperor, took refuge at the Safavid court in 1544 and recovered his throne with Tahmasp's soldiers. Pari Khan Khanum, the shah's daughter, emerged in his final years as a court power broker. The Battle of Jam in 1528 saw the fourteen-year-old shah defeat the Uzbek khan Ubayd Allah with gunpowder weapons. The move of the capital to Qazvin, around 1548, reshaped the geography of Safavid power. The Sincere Repentance edict of the early 1530s marked the beginning of Tahmasp's turn to sober piety.

Analysis

Tahmasp's reign is a lesson in the value of endurance. He won no great battles of conquest. He added little territory. He was not remembered by his contemporaries, and is rarely remembered now, as a charismatic figure. What he did was harder and less glamorous: he refused to lose. Year after year, decade after decade, he absorbed blows, ceded ground when he had to, retreated to fight another season, and outlasted the men who tried to destroy him.

His strategic logic was defensive in the best sense. By moving the capital inland, he denied the Ottomans a decisive target. By negotiating Amasya, he converted a bleeding stalemate into a stable peace. By building up his household of *ghulam* slaves, he planted the seed of an institution that would one day free the monarchy from Qizilbash blackmail. By patronizing Shi'a clerics and codifying religious practice, he transformed a volatile ideology into an enduring civic faith. Each of these moves was incremental. Together they saved the empire.

Quick Summary

- Tahmasp I inherited the throne at age ten in 1524 and reigned for fifty-two years, the longest in Safavid history.

- His early reign was dominated by Qizilbash civil wars among rival Turkmen factions competing to control the child king.

- At fourteen he defeated the Uzbeks at the Battle of Jam in 1528, using gunpowder weapons to telling effect.

- Around 1548 he moved the capital from exposed Tabriz to more defensible Qazvin, reshaping the geography of Safavid rule.

- Three Ottoman invasions under Suleiman the Magnificent ended with the Peace of Amasya in 1555, which held for over thirty years.

- In 1544 he sheltered the exiled Mughal emperor Humayun and provided the army that helped him recover his throne.

- His Sincere Repentance in the early 1530s banned wine and entertainment, signaling a shift toward clerical, legalistic Shi'ism.

- He died in 1576, leaving a stronger state but no clear heir, triggering a violent succession crisis.

When historians list the great Safavid shahs, Tahmasp rarely tops the page. Ismail founded the dynasty; Abbas glorified it. Tahmasp merely kept it going. But keeping it going was the decisive act. Without his patience, without the fifty-two years in which Iran learned to be a

Shi'a state at peace with itself and at bearable tension with its neighbors, there would have been no empire left for Abbas to beautify. The Crimson Crown survived its second generation because a quiet, devout boy grew into a stubborn, watchful king and refused, year after year, to let it fall.

Tahmasp kept the dynasty going, year by watchful year, and in doing so he handed his successors a kingdom. But he also handed them the problem his father had left him, unresolved and increasingly dangerous: a tribal aristocracy that believed itself divinely authorized to choose, unmake, and occasionally murder its own shahs. The men in red caps had carried Ismail to Tabriz and held the line through Tahmasp's long reign. They were indispensable. They were also, from the throne's point of view, intolerable. How to keep the first quality while defusing the second was the defining political question of the Safavid century.

Chapter 6:

The Qizilbash and the Crown

They wore scarlet caps with twelve folds, one for each of the Shi'a Imams, and they believed their master was something close to God on earth. Without them, there would have been no Safavid Empire. With them, no Safavid Shah could ever sleep entirely soundly.

The Qizilbash - the "Red Heads" - were the hammer that forged the Persian state. Turkic, tribal, ferocious, and bound to the house of Ismail by a devotion that bordered on worship, they had ridden out of Anatolia and the Caucasus to topple the Aq Qoyunlu in 1501 and conquer a kingdom for a teenage messiah. Yet within a generation of that triumph, the same warriors who had made the dynasty became its principal danger. They quarreled, they intrigued, they murdered one another in palace corridors, and on more than one occasion they murdered the very king they were sworn to defend. The story of the Safavid sixteenth and seventeenth centuries is, in large part, the story of how the Shahs slowly, painfully, and cleverly broke the power of the men who had crowned them - replacing tribal cavalry with Persian clerks and Caucasian slaves, and in the process inventing a new kind of Iranian state.

Tribal Confederations and the Twelve Tassels

To understand the Qizilbash, begin with the cap. It was a tall, conical headdress wound with a turban, distinguished by twelve red gores or tassels that announced allegiance to the Twelve Imams of Shi'a Islam. Sheikh Heydar, Ismail's father, is credited with imposing it on his followers in the late fifteenth century, and from that moment the headgear became a kind of uniform - and, for the Sunni Ottomans across the border, a provocation visible from a hundred paces.

The men beneath those caps were not Persians. They were Turkmen, drawn from a constellation of tribes scattered across eastern Anatolia, northern Syria, Azerbaijan, and the highlands stretching toward the Caspian. Seven groups dominated the early confederation: the Shamlu, Ustajlu, Takkalu, Rumlu, Dhu'l-Qadr, Afshar, and Qajar. Each had its own pasturelands, its own chieftains, its own sense of ancient honor. What bound them together was not blood but devotion - to the Safaviyya Sufi order and, above all, to the charismatic family that led it.

That devotion ran deep enough to be uncomfortable. Qizilbash poetry composed in Ismail's name addressed the young Shah as the reincarnation of Ali, as the Mahdi, sometimes simply as God. Warriors were said to ride into battle without armor, certain that their *murshid-i kamil*, their perfect spiritual guide, would shield them from harm. At Chaldiran in 1514 this belief was tested by Ottoman cannon and found wanting. But the underlying theology survived the catastrophe. The Shah was not merely a king; he was the visible representative of the Hidden Imam, and to serve him was to serve salvation itself.

This was the genius of the Safavid project, and also its built-in instability. A tribal warrior who believes his king is divine will fight for him to the death. But that same warrior will also believe he has a personal, almost mystical claim on the king's favor - and on the offices, lands, and revenues that flow from royal favor. Multiply this conviction across seven proud tribes, each jealous of the others, each convinced its devotion was the truest, and you have a powder keg.

The administrative geography of the early empire reflected the bargain. The great provincial governorships - Herat, Shirvan, Azerbaijan, Fars, Kerman - were parceled out to Qizilbash chiefs, who held them as *uymaqs*, tribal appanages, with the right to collect taxes, raise troops, and tutor royal princes. In effect, Ismail had conquered Iran by promising to share it. The princes he sent to the provinces were placed under the guardianship of a tribal *lala*, or tutor, whose loyalty to his ward could swiftly become a weapon against the throne. The crown sat atop the tribes; it did not yet sit above them.

Loyalty, Rebellion, and Royal Murder

Ismail's death in 1524 exposed the flaw in the design with brutal clarity. His heir, Tahmasp, was ten years old. For the next decade the empire was effectively governed by whichever Qizilbash faction had managed to seize the boy and dominate the court. The Ustajlu and the Shamlu went to war with each other in the streets of Tabriz. Chiefs were assassinated, others fled to the Ottomans, others to the Uzbeks. Provincial governors stopped remitting taxes. The Ottoman sultan Suleyman, watching from Istanbul, marched east and helped himself to Baghdad and much of Iraq.

Tahmasp, when at last he came of age, never forgot. His long reign of more than half a century became a slow, careful campaign to play the tribes against one another, shifting governorships, manufacturing rivalries, executing a chief here and elevating an upstart there. He survived. The empire survived. But the underlying structure - a Turkmen military aristocracy on whose continued cooperation the dynasty depended - did not change.

When Tahmasp died in 1576, the cycle began again, with interest. The succession crisis that followed was a slaughter. His son Ismail II, released from twenty years of imprisonment in the fortress of Qahqaha, set about murdering his own brothers and half-brothers with such enthusiasm that the Qizilbash chiefs around him concluded he had to go. Within two years he was dead, almost certainly poisoned, possibly by his own sister. His successor, the half-blind Mohammad Khodabanda, was a figurehead. Real power passed to a swirl of Qizilbash factions whose feuds spilled blood from Qazvin to Khorasan.

The body count tells the story. Royal princes were strangled in their cradles. Queens, including Khodabanda's formidable wife Khayr al-Nisa Begum, were murdered in the harem - in her case by a delegation of Qizilbash chiefs who simply walked into her chambers and killed her for the offense of trying to govern. Provincial governors raised armies and marched on the capital. The Ottomans, sensing weakness, invaded again and seized Tabriz. The Uzbeks did the same in the east.

By the time the sixteen-year-old Abbas was hoisted onto the throne in 1588 - his own father deposed by the same Qizilbash who had set him up - the empire was bleeding from every frontier, and the throne itself had become a chair on which no man could safely sit. The young Shah inherited a state in which the men sworn to die for him had killed his mother, blinded his brother, deposed his father, and now expected him to be grateful.

He was not grateful. He was patient, and he was furious, and he had a plan.

The Rise of the Tajik Bureaucracy

The plan had two halves. The first was old; the second was new. Together they would remake the Iranian state.

The old half was the Tajik bureaucracy. "Tajik" in Safavid usage did not yet mean an ethnic group in the modern sense; it meant a Persian-speaker, a man of the settled cities and irrigated valleys, a scribe rather than a warrior. The Persian administrative class was older than Islam itself. Its forebears had run the chanceries of the Sasanians, the Abbasids, the Seljuks, the Mongols, and the Timurids. Empires came and went; the scribes remained, drafting tax registers in the same elegant hand, computing land assessments by the same methods, quoting the same poets in the margins of the same legal documents.

The Safavids, like every dynasty before them, could not function without these men. From the start, the highest civil offices of the state - the *vizier*, the *mustawfi al-mamalik* (chief comptroller), the *sadr* who supervised religious endowments - were held by Persians of distinguished family, often from old houses in Isfahan, Shiraz, Yazd, or Qazvin. They drafted the decrees that the Shah sealed. They calculated the revenues that paid the Qizilbash. They corresponded in florid Persian with the courts of Delhi, Istanbul, and Bukhara.

What changed under Tahmasp and accelerated under Abbas was the political weight of these officials. As long as provinces were held as tribal appanages, the chancery's writ stopped at the borders of the *uymaq*. The Qizilbash chief in Herat collected his own taxes, paid his own troops, and answered to the Shah only when it suited him. But if a province could be converted into *khasseh* - crown land administered directly by royal officials - then the revenues flowed to the treasury and the men who counted them became indispensable.

Abbas converted province after province. Gilan, Mazandaran, Yazd, Kerman, eventually much of Isfahan's hinterland - all were pulled out of tribal hands and into the bureaucratic machine. Each conversion meant new positions for Persian administrators: tax collectors, judges, irrigation overseers, market inspectors. The men who held these positions did not raise armies. They did not have ancestral pasturelands. They could not appeal to Sufi devotion or tribal honor. They held their offices entirely at the Shah's pleasure, and they knew it.

This was a different kind of power than the Qizilbash had ever wielded, and it was more durable precisely because it was so dependent. A great Persian vizier could fall in an afternoon - dozens did - but the office and the apparatus survived him. The bureaucracy was a body without a head, which meant the Shah could always supply a new head without losing the body. The tribal confederations, by contrast, were heads without bodies: kill the chief, and the tribe still existed, still grazed its flocks, still nursed its grievances.

Yet bureaucrats alone could not fight the Ottomans. For that, Abbas needed soldiers. And the soldiers he chose to build his new army were drawn from a source that no Qizilbash chieftain could rival or even imitate.

Slaves of the Shah: The Ghulam System

They were called *ghulaman-i khasseh-yi sharifeh* - slaves of the noble royal household - and they were the cleverest single innovation of Shah Abbas's reign.

The model was not original. The Ottomans had their Janissaries, recruited as Christian boys from the Balkans, converted, trained, and turned into the sultan's personal infantry. The medieval Mamluks of Egypt had built an entire ruling caste from imported slave soldiers. Abbas, who watched the Ottomans closely and learned from them constantly, adapted the principle to Iranian conditions and Iranian frontiers.

His raw material came from the Caucasus. The campaigns he launched into Georgia, Armenia, and Circassia in the 1590s and early 1600s brought back tens of thousands of captives - boys and young men from Christian villages, taken often in their early teens, marched south to Isfahan, and inducted into the royal household. They were converted to Shi'a Islam. They were taught Persian. They were trained in arms, in horsemanship, in the elaborate etiquette of the court. And then they were given jobs.

The jobs were extraordinary. Ghulams commanded regiments. They governed provinces - by the end of Abbas's reign, perhaps a fifth of all governorships were in their hands, including such plums as Fars, Kerman, and Astarabad. They served as chamberlains, treasurers, masters of the horse, ambassadors. The most successful - men like Allahverdi Khan, a Georgian convert who rose to be commander-in-chief of all Safavid forces and effectively the second man in the empire - amassed fortunes and dynastic influence that rivaled anything the old Qizilbash families had ever known.

What made the ghulams so useful was precisely what made them so vulnerable. They had no tribe. They had no homeland to flee to, no kinsmen to shelter rebellious instincts, no ancestral devotion to a Sufi order that predated the dynasty. Their entire existence - their faith, their language, their wealth, their station - was the gift of the Shah. Treason was not merely dangerous; it was unthinkable, because there was no community to defect to. A disgraced Qizilbash chief could ride to the Ottoman frontier and be welcomed; a disgraced ghulam had nowhere to go.

Abbas paired the ghulams with another innovation: firearms. With help from the English Sherley brothers, who arrived at his court in 1598, he reorganized his army to include musket-armed infantry (*tofangchis*) and a powerful artillery corps (*tupchis*), most of them recruited from outside the Qizilbash tribes. By 1600 the new royal army numbered tens of thousands of professionals, paid in cash from the treasury that the Tajik bureaucrats now filled. The traditional tribal cavalry remained essential, but it no longer monopolized the means of violence. The Shah, for the first time, possessed a standing force that owed everything to him personally.

The results showed quickly. Between 1603 and 1623, Abbas recovered Tabriz, Baghdad, Mosul, Mesopotamia, and Hormuz - territories that had been bleeding away for half a century. The Ottoman frontier, which had crept eastward under his predecessors, was driven back to where Ismail had held it. The Uzbeks were thrown out of Khorasan. The empire, which a generation earlier had looked to be dying, was suddenly larger, richer, and more centralized than it had ever been.

Behind every one of those victories stood ghulam commanders and bureaucratic financiers - and a Qizilbash establishment that was finding itself, year by year, edged a little further from the center of power.

A New Composite Elite

Abbas did not destroy the Qizilbash. They remained the largest single bloc of his cavalry to the end of his reign, and tribal chiefs continued to hold great offices and lead armies in the field. What he did was more subtle and more lasting: he turned a single-pillar regime into a three-pillar one.

By the 1620s the Safavid state rested on three distinct and mutually suspicious elites. The Qizilbash supplied tribal cavalry and a residual claim to spiritual partnership with the dynasty. The Tajiks supplied the pen, the ledger, and the institutional memory of Persian statecraft. The ghulams supplied loyal soldiers, trustworthy governors, and a closed cadre of men whose entire identity was wrapped around the throne. None could function without the others. None could overthrow the others. And the Shah, sitting at the apex, could play any one of the three against the remaining two.

This was the architecture that allowed the Safavid state to outlive its turbulent youth and become, for a century, one of the great powers of Asia. It also, eventually, produced its own pathologies. Ghulam factions would learn to intrigue as ruthlessly as any Qizilbash chief had ever done. The harem, where so many ghulams had begun their careers, would in time become the principal arena of political combat. And the very stability that the three-pillar system bought would breed a complacency, a fixedness, that left later Shahs ill-equipped for shocks they could not foresee.

But that lay in the future. In the early seventeenth century, with Isfahan rising as the most beautiful city in the Islamic world and the empire's frontiers expanding outward, Abbas had achieved what Tahmasp had only dreamed of. He had broken the Qizilbash without destroying them. He had made the crown, at last, weigh more than the caps that had once placed it on his ancestor's head.

Key Figures & Events

Sheikh Heydar gave the Qizilbash their distinctive twelve-folded red cap in the late fifteenth century, transforming a Sufi brotherhood into a recognizable military movement. Shah Ismail I rode that movement to power in 1501, but his death in 1524 unleashed a decade of tribal civil war that nearly destroyed the dynasty. Shah Tahmasp survived by cunning rather than reform; the succession crises after his death in 1576 produced a bloodbath in which queens, princes, and Shahs alike were murdered by Qizilbash factions.

Shah Abbas I, enthroned at sixteen in 1588, broke the cycle by building two parallel power structures: an expanded Tajik bureaucracy that ran an enlarged crown domain, and a corps of converted Caucasian slave-soldiers, the ghulams, who staffed his new standing army and, increasingly, his governorates. Allahverdi Khan, a Georgian ghulam who rose to command all Safavid forces, embodied the new order. Together with the English adventurers Anthony and Robert Sherley, who helped modernize Iranian artillery and musketry, the ghulams gave Abbas the military edge to recover Tabriz, Baghdad, and Hormuz between 1603 and 1623.

Analysis

The transformation of the Safavid military and administrative elite is one of the great case studies in early modern state-building - and a mirror image of what was happening in Ottoman Istanbul, Mughal Agra, and even, in different form, in the France of Louis XIII. Across Eurasia, the seventeenth century saw monarchs strain to subordinate hereditary warrior aristocracies to centralized fiscal-military states staffed by professionals who served at the ruler's pleasure.

What made the Iranian version distinctive was its raw material. The Safavids had no Balkan hinterland to draw on, no provincial nobility willing to sell its sons into royal service. They had the Caucasus, and they had a religious ideology - Twelver Shi'ism - that made conversion the price of advancement. The result was a ruling class that was, by the 1620s, astonishingly diverse: Turkmen tribal lords, Persian scribes from ancient urban families, and Georgian and Circassian converts whose grandparents had been Christian peasants. What held them together was not ethnicity, not language, not even religion in any deep sense, but the common service of the Shah and the elaborate ceremonial culture of his court.

That, in the end, was the achievement. Ismail had founded a state on tribal devotion. Abbas refounded it on royal service. The crown was no longer the tallest cap among many; it was a sovereignty that stood above caps altogether.

Quick Summary

- The Qizilbash were Turkmen tribal warriors whose twelve-folded red caps signaled devotion to the Twelve Imams and to the Safavid family as quasi-divine spiritual masters.

- Seven major tribes - Shamlu, Ustajlu, Takkalu, Rumlu, Dhu'l-Qadr, Afshar, and Qajar - dominated the early empire, holding provinces as tribal appanages and tutoring royal princes.

- Succession crises in 1524 and 1576 unleashed tribal civil wars in which queens, princes, and Shahs were murdered by rival Qizilbash factions.

- Shah Abbas I (r. 1588-1629) responded by expanding the Persian Tajik bureaucracy and converting tribal provinces into directly administered crown lands.

- He built a corps of ghulams - converted slave-soldiers from the Christian Caucasus - who staffed a new standing army equipped with firearms and artillery.

- Ghulams could rise to the highest commands and governorships; the Georgian Allahverdi Khan became commander-in-chief of all Safavid forces.

- By the 1620s the empire rested on three pillars - Qizilbash, Tajiks, and ghulams - allowing the Shah to balance them against one another.

- The reforms enabled Abbas to recover Tabriz, Baghdad, and Hormuz and to make Isfahan one of the great cities of the world.

The taming of the Qizilbash was not a single dramatic event but a slow renegotiation of what it meant to rule Iran. The men in red caps did not vanish; they were absorbed, balanced, outflanked. In their place rose something the Iranian plateau had not seen since the fall of the Sasanians: a centralized monarchy that drew its servants from every corner of the known world and answered, at least in theory, to no one but the Shah. That settlement would carry the Safavids to their zenith - and, when it eventually frayed, would carry them swiftly toward their fall.

The settlement that would eventually absorb, balance, and outflank the Qizilbash did not arrive on schedule. Before a centralized monarchy could emerge from the tribal confederation, the confederation had to break itself against the limits of its own logic. When Tahmasp died in 1576 with nine sons and no clear succession, the question of who could rightfully choose a Safavid shah came due all at once. The answer, delivered over eleven years of poisonings and factional war, was almost no one. The empire that survived those years survived barely, and only by learning, at ruinous cost, that it could not continue as it had been.

Chapter 7:

The Lost Decades

When Shah Tahmasp died in May 1576, he left behind nine sons, a treasury stuffed with silver, and an empire that would nearly devour itself within a decade.

The eleven years between Tahmasp's death and the coronation of his grandson Abbas in 1587 are the hinge on which Safavid history turns. Had the dynasty collapsed in those years - and it came astonishingly close - the map of western Asia would look very different today. Instead, the empire endured a spasm of fratricide, poisonings, factional warfare, and foreign invasion before producing, almost by accident, the greatest shah in its history. What follows traces that long unraveling: the paranoid eighteen-month reign of Ismail II, the puppet kingship of the half-blind Mohammad Khodabanda, the assassination of two royal women who tried to hold the center, the Ottoman seizure of Tabriz in 1585, and the quiet conspiracy in Khorasan that produced a sixteen-year-old shah. The Qizilbash tribes, once the shock troops of the revolution, became the wreckers of it. Their rivalries turned the throne into a prize to be fought over rather than an institution to be served. That everything held together at all owed less to Safavid genius than to Ottoman distraction and a handful of provincial strongmen with patience enough to wait.

Ismail II: The Imprisoned Prince Becomes Shah

For twenty years, Ismail Mirza had lived in a cell in the mountain fortress of Qahqaha, west of Qazvin. His crime had been ambiguous - a mixture of military success, popularity with the Qizilbash, and suspected plotting against his father. Tahmasp had preferred imprisonment to execution. When the old shah died, Ismail was forty years old, hardened, bitter, and addicted to opium.

The succession itself was a knife fight conducted in whispers. Tahmasp had shown no clear preference among his sons. One faction at court, led by the powerful princess Pari Khan Khanum - Tahmasp's favorite daughter and a formidable political operator in her own right - backed Ismail. Another faction pushed his younger brother Haydar. The contest was decided within hours of Tahmasp's last breath. Haydar was cornered in the harem at Qazvin and killed. Pari Khan Khanum's allies dispatched riders to Qahqaha. Ismail was brought down from his mountain and placed on the throne in August 1576.

What followed was a reign so grim that contemporary chroniclers, themselves accustomed to royal cruelty, struggled to describe it without flinching. Ismail II seems to have emerged from his long captivity convinced that every male relative was a future rival. He set about eliminating them. Within months, he had ordered the execution or blinding of most of his brothers and nephews. Sultan Ibrahim Mirza, a poet and patron of painters who had overseen one of the most beautiful workshops of the age, was strangled. Others were hunted down in the provinces. Only two of Tahmasp's sons survived the purge with their lives and eyes intact: Mohammad Khodabanda, spared because his weak eyesight made him appear harmless, and the infant Abbas, hidden by loyal guardians in distant Herat.

Ismail's other obsession was religious. He had been raised in the fierce Shia milieu of his father's court, but during his years in prison he appears to have drifted toward Sunni sympathies, or at least toward a distaste for the more extreme devotional practices - the public cursing of the first three caliphs, the theatrical displays of Ali worship - that had become hallmarks of Qizilbash piety. As shah, he tried to rein these practices in. He ordered the removal of the names of the Twelve Imams from coinage. He replaced Shia preachers with more orthodox clerics. The Qizilbash chiefs who had put him on the throne watched, appalled, as he attacked the very ideology that justified their power.

He ignored them. He also ignored Pari Khan Khanum, whose support had been decisive and who now found herself shut out of a court she had expected to dominate. He ignored, too, the business of government itself, withdrawing into his harem with his opium and his fears. Provincial governors went unappointed. Petitions piled up unread. Only the executions continued.

On the night of 24 November 1577, Ismail II was found dead in his bed. He had spent the previous evening wandering the streets of Qazvin in disguise, returning in the small hours with an associate. The official cause was an overdose of opium mixed with something stronger. Few believed it was accidental. Pari Khan Khanum was widely thought to have arranged the poisoning, and she was the one who moved first to name a successor. Whether she killed him or not, she certainly inherited him. Ismail had reigned for barely fifteen months and left behind an empire traumatized, a dynasty gutted, and a treasury still, remarkably, intact.

Khodabanda and the Regency of Mahd-e Olya

The new shah was chosen for his weakness. Mohammad Khodabanda - the name means "slave of God" - was Tahmasp's eldest surviving son, nearly blind from an illness in youth, gentle-natured, uninterested in rule. He had spent the purge years as governor of Shiraz, cultivating poets and ignoring politics. Pari Khan Khanum summoned him to Qazvin confident that she could govern through him while he composed verses in a darkened room.

She miscalculated. Khodabanda arrived in early 1578 accompanied by his wife, Khayr al-Nisa Begum, known by her title Mahd-e Olya, "the Sublime Cradle." Mahd-e Olya was a princess of the Mazandaran ruling family, intelligent, ambitious, and entirely uninterested in sharing power with her sister-in-law. Within days of the coronation, Pari Khan Khanum was dead. She was strangled in her own apartments, on orders widely attributed to Mahd-e Olya, and her body was displayed to silence any lingering partisans. The woman who had made two shahs was disposed of before she could make a third.

Mahd-e Olya then did something remarkable: she ruled. Her husband nominally sat on the throne, but every document of consequence passed through her hands. She appointed governors, conducted correspondence with foreign powers, issued decrees, and reviewed military dispatches. For roughly a year and a half, the Safavid Empire was governed by a queen in everything but title. Contemporary observers, Persian and European alike, recognized her as the real sovereign. The Venetian bailo in Istanbul reported that the Shah "sees little and decides nothing," while his wife "commands all."

This was intolerable to the Qizilbash. The tribal chiefs had accepted Khodabanda precisely because they expected to dominate him. A woman's regency, and a non-Qizilbash woman at that, threatened everything they had assumed they were gaining. Matters grew worse when Mahd-e Olya began promoting Tajik administrators and Persian-speaking bureaucrats over the Turkic tribal elite. She understood, as her husband did not, that the Qizilbash were the problem rather than the solution - but understanding a problem is not the same as solving it.

In July 1579, a group of Qizilbash amirs forced their way into the harem at Qazvin. They confronted Mahd-e Olya with accusations - some political, some designed to humiliate, including alleged intrigues with Adil Giray, a captive Crimean prince held at the Safavid court. The queen denied everything. Her husband, informed of the incursion, sent word that he could not intervene. The amirs strangled her. They then dragged her body to the palace gates and left it there as a warning.

Khodabanda wept and did nothing. The message was unmistakable: the shah was a figurehead, the Qizilbash were the state, and any attempt to govern around them would end in murder. The years that followed saw the amirs plunder provincial revenues, settle personal scores under the color of royal authority, and fight each other for control of the young princes who represented the future. Into this vacuum the Ottomans now stepped.

Ottoman Invasion and the Loss of the Caucasus

Sultan Murad III had been watching Safavid disintegration with the attentiveness of a card player seeing his opponent's hand. The peace of Amasya, concluded with Tahmasp in 1555, had held for two decades. It was now worth less than the paper it was written on. In 1578, even as Mahd-e Olya was still alive, Ottoman armies crossed the frontier.

The strategic logic was straightforward. The Caucasus - Georgia, Shirvan, Dagestan, parts of Armenia - was a region of mountain kingdoms and fortified towns nominally under Safavid suzerainty, in practice contested between the two empires. With the Safavids paralyzed, the Ottomans could absorb the whole area at comparatively low cost. The campaign was entrusted to Lala Mustafa Pasha, an experienced commander who had served in Cyprus.

Ottoman forces moved in multiple columns. One drove through eastern Anatolia toward the Georgian kingdoms; another pushed into Shirvan along the Caspian coast. Safavid resistance was brave but uncoordinated. Qizilbash contingents, still fighting well at the tactical level, found themselves unsupported. Commanders quarreled over precedence. Supplies arrived late or not at all. Tbilisi fell. Shirvan was overrun. By 1580, the Ottomans had reached the Caspian.

The Crimean Tatars, Ottoman vassals, added their own weight to the offensive by raiding southward across the steppe. For a time it seemed the Safavids might lose not just the Caucasus but Azerbaijan itself. A young Qizilbash officer named Imam Quli Khan - not to be confused with the later general of the same name - wrote to Qazvin begging for reinforcements that never came. The court was too busy with its own quarrels.

The worst blow came in 1585. Tabriz - the original Safavid capital, the city where Ismail I had proclaimed his faith in 1501, the symbolic heart of the empire - fell to Ottoman forces under Özdemiroğlu Osman Pasha. The Ottomans found the city half-evacuated and looted what remained. They built a massive citadel to hold it. Tabriz had been taken by the Ottomans before, briefly, but this occupation would last over a decade. For Persians of the period, the loss felt civilizational, not merely military. A chronicle of the event describes the city's inhabitants fleeing into the hills "carrying nothing but the memory of what had been."

To the east, the Uzbeks took the opportunity to raid Khorasan, probing Safavid defenses around Mashhad and Herat. The empire was now losing ground on two fronts simultaneously while its shah sat nearly blind in Qazvin and its generals plotted against each other. Something had to give.

The Khorasan Faction and Young Prince Abbas

What gave, finally, was the fiction that the crown belonged to Mohammad Khodabanda.

For several years, a quiet reorganization had been taking place in the northeast. Prince Abbas, Khodabanda's third son, had been installed as nominal governor of Khorasan while still a boy. His effective guardians were two powerful Qizilbash chiefs, Murshid Quli Khan of the Ustajlu tribe and Ali Quli Khan of the Shamlu tribe. For a while these two men were rivals; eventually Murshid Quli eliminated his colleague and concentrated authority over the prince in his own hands.

Abbas grew up in Herat and Mashhad, far from the poisoned atmosphere of Qazvin. He was educated in Persian literature and Shia theology, trained in horsemanship and archery, and - crucially - exposed from childhood to the practical problems of governing a frontier province under constant Uzbek pressure. By 1587 he was sixteen, slight, dark-eyed, intelligent, and already known for a temper that could flash into violence. He had also learned, the hard way, that his own Qizilbash protectors were not entirely his friends.

Murshid Quli Khan's calculation was simple. Khodabanda was finished. The empire was hemorrhaging territory. Another of Khodabanda's sons, Hamza Mirza, had briefly seemed a promising heir apparent - he had led troops competently against the Ottomans - but in December 1586 he was assassinated in his camp, probably by Qizilbash rivals. With Hamza dead, Abbas was the obvious successor. Whoever controlled Abbas would control the next reign.

In the summer of 1587, Murshid Quli Khan moved. He marched west from Khorasan with a small but disciplined force and with the prince riding beside him. They crossed the Dasht-e Kavir in the late heat, a march of calculated audacity, and approached Qazvin before the court there had assembled a response. Other Qizilbash factions, exhausted by a decade of civil strife and faced with Ottoman armies in their own provinces, chose not to oppose him. Some actively welcomed the change. Khodabanda, informed that his son was at the gates, did what he had done throughout his reign: he acquiesced.

Coup at Qazvin, 1587

The transfer of power, when it came, was almost anticlimactic. On 1 October 1587, Abbas entered Qazvin at the head of Murshid Quli Khan's troops. He went directly to the palace. Khodabanda met his son, embraced him, and formally placed the royal turban on his head. The ex-shah was neither killed nor blinded - a rare mercy in Safavid succession politics - but retired into private life, where he would live on for another decade in obscurity.

Murshid Quli Khan assumed the title of vakil, regent and chief minister, fully expecting to govern in the young shah's name as others had done before him. He settled into his new eminence with satisfaction. He had made a king; he would now enjoy the making.

Abbas allowed this for exactly as long as it took him to learn the palace, memorize the names of the tribal chiefs, and identify which of them hated which. The education lasted about a year. In July 1589,

Murshid Quli Khan was summoned to a private audience and executed - on the shah's direct order, by men the shah had personally chosen. The regent joined the long list of Qizilbash kingmakers who had discovered, too late, that making kings is a perilous trade.

With that single killing, Abbas served notice. The Qizilbash era of the Safavid state was ending. A different empire was about to be built - centralized, cosmopolitan, dependent on new military corps recruited from Caucasian converts rather than Turkic tribesmen, and financed by reforms of breathtaking ambition. That story belongs to the next chapter. It began on the day in October 1587 when a sixteen-year-old accepted a turban in Qazvin and decided, silently, that he would not be the puppet anyone expected.

Key Figures & Events

Ismail II (r. 1576-1577): Released from twenty years' imprisonment to take the throne. Purged his male relatives, flirted with Sunni orthodoxy, and died of suspected poisoning within fifteen months.

Pari Khan Khanum (d. 1578): Daughter of Tahmasp, political architect of Ismail II's accession and probable author of his death. Strangled within days of Khodabanda's coronation.

Mohammad Khodabanda (r. 1578-1587): Near-blind elder prince, installed as a figurehead, deposed by his own son. One of the few Safavid ex-shahs to die in bed.

Mahd-e Olya (d. 1579): Khodabanda's queen, effective ruler for eighteen months, murdered in her harem by Qizilbash chiefs who would not accept a woman's government.

Murshid Quli Khan (d. 1589): Ustajlu chief who engineered the coup of 1587 and was executed two years later by the shah he had enthroned.

The Fall of Tabriz (1585): Ottoman capture of the old Safavid capital, a psychological blow as much as a strategic one.

Analysis

The lost decades expose a structural flaw in the early Safavid state. Ismail I had built his empire on the devotion of Turkic tribal warriors who saw him as a messianic figure; Tahmasp had managed these warriors by playing them against each other and by the sheer length of his own reign. Neither had solved the underlying problem: the Qizilbash owed primary loyalty to their tribes rather than to the throne, and a weak shah simply meant tribal civil war.

When Tahmasp died, the machinery failed catastrophically. Pari Khan Khanum and Mahd-e Olya both tried, in different ways, to govern around the Qizilbash; both were murdered. Khodabanda surrendered to them and lost half the empire. Only Abbas, who had grown up watching the system from its most contested frontier, understood that reform had to mean replacement - the Qizilbash themselves would have to be broken as a political force.

That the dynasty survived at all was partly luck. The Ottomans were simultaneously fighting the Habsburgs and managing troubles on the Danube. The Uzbeks were divided among themselves. Had either adversary been able to concentrate against Iran in the early 1580s, the Safavid state might have ended there, remembered as a brief Shia interlude between Sunni empires. Instead, the system held - just - long enough for a teenager in Khorasan to inherit what remained of it and to do something extraordinary with the inheritance.

Quick Summary

- Shah Tahmasp died in 1576 after a 52-year reign, triggering a succession crisis among his nine sons.

- Ismail II, released from two decades of imprisonment, purged his relatives, favored Sunni orthodoxy, and died in suspected poisoning after fifteen months.

- Pari Khan Khanum, Tahmasp's politically gifted daughter, was murdered by agents of Queen Mahd-e Olya shortly after Khodabanda's coronation.

- Mahd-e Olya effectively ruled for eighteen months before being strangled by Qizilbash chiefs in 1579.

- Ottoman armies exploited the chaos, seizing Georgia, Shirvan, and finally Tabriz itself in 1585.

- Prince Abbas, raised in Khorasan under the guardianship of Murshid Quli Khan, was brought to Qazvin in a bloodless coup in 1587.

- Khodabanda abdicated peacefully; Murshid Quli Khan was executed by Abbas two years later.

- The crisis exposed the Qizilbash tribal system as the central weakness of the Safavid state, setting the agenda for Abbas's later reforms.

The eleven years from 1576 to 1587 were, in retrospect, the near-death of the Safavid project. The empire that emerged from them was wounded, shrunken, and bitterly educated. It was also, for the first time, ready to become something other than a Qizilbash confederation with a shah on top. The next chapter follows the young man who walked into Qazvin in October 1587 as he turned that readiness into one of the most remarkable reigns in Iranian history.

Eleven years of near-collapse had taught the Safavid state a single lesson it could not unlearn: the Qizilbash confederation with a shah on top could not endure. What it would become instead was not yet decided. That decision would be made by the young man who walked into Qazvin in October 1587, sixteen years old and the puppet of the warlord who had killed his mother. He had inherited a shrunken, wounded empire and the bitter education of the lost decades. He would turn both into the raw material of a reign that later generations, reaching for a word large enough, would simply call great.

Chapter 8:

Abbas the Great

He was sixteen years old, the son of a half-blind shah, and the puppet of the very warlord who had murdered his mother and elder brother. Within a year he would have that warlord killed in a roadside ambush. Within a decade he would remake the army, the treasury, and the map of Iran.

Shah Abbas I came to the throne in 1588 inheriting a state on the edge of dissolution. Ottoman armies had swept through the western provinces. Uzbek raiders had carved up Khorasan in the east. The Qizilbash tribes - the red-capped Turkmen warriors who had carried his great-grandfather Ismail to power - had spent two decades fighting one another for control of weak shahs, and now treated the throne as their property. The empire founded with such ferocity in 1501 had become, by the 1580s, a wreckage of feuding chieftains and lost frontiers. Over the next forty-one years, Abbas would reverse all of it. He would build a standing army of slave-soldiers loyal only to him, smash the tribal aristocracy that had dominated Safavid politics for a century, drive out the Ottomans and Uzbeks, and turn his new capital at Isfahan into one of the great cities of the seventeenth-century world. He would also, in his old age, blind one son and execute another. The man who saved the Safavid state was, by any honest reckoning, both its most brilliant ruler and its most dangerous.

Securing the Throne

The coup that brought Abbas to power was not his own. In the autumn of 1587, Murshid Quli Khan, governor of Mashhad and head of the Ustajlu Qizilbash, marched the young prince out of Khorasan and into the Safavid heartland. By the spring of 1588 the reigning shah,

Mohammad Khodabanda, half-blind and worn down by tribal infighting, had been quietly pushed aside. Abbas, all of sixteen, was crowned at Qazvin.

For roughly a year, Murshid Quli Khan governed in his name. The new shah attended council, signed decrees, and watched. He was learning who his enemies were, and who could be turned. The Qizilbash had killed his mother, Khayr al-Nisa Begum, in 1579 because she had tried to govern in her husband's place. They had killed his elder brother Hamza in 1586. Abbas had no illusions about the men who had placed the crown on his head. They were the same men who had murdered his family.

In July 1589, on the road outside Qazvin, Murshid Quli Khan was cut down by assassins acting on the shah's order. Abbas was now ruling alone, and ruling at seventeen. The killing was a signal, brutal and unmistakable, to every tribal grandee in the empire: the era in which Qizilbash kingmakers chose, controlled, and disposed of shahs was over.

Yet a signal was not the same as a solution. The empire he now governed in name was scarcely his to command. Tabriz, the original Safavid capital, was in Ottoman hands. Mashhad and Herat had fallen to the Uzbek khan Abdullah II. The provincial governorships - Fars, Kerman, Azerbaijan, the Caspian rim - were held by tribal chieftains who collected their own taxes, raised their own troops, and answered to no one in particular. The treasury at Qazvin was nearly empty.

Abbas made a decision that defined the rest of his reign: before he could fight outward, he had to fight inward. He sued the Ottomans for peace in 1590, signing the humiliating Treaty of Istanbul that ceded Tabriz, Shirvan, Georgia, and large stretches of Luristan. Contemporaries were aghast. Abbas was buying time, and he knew exactly what he intended to buy with it.

That same year he moved his court south, eventually settling on Isfahan as the new capital. The choice was deliberate. Isfahan lay deep in the Persian-speaking interior, far from the Qizilbash power bases of the northwest, surrounded by fertile plains, and astride the trade routes linking the Persian Gulf to Central Asia. From Isfahan, the shah could be reached by tribal lords only with effort. From Isfahan, the shah could reach everywhere else. It was a capital chosen by a young man who intended to centralize an empire, and who already knew how he meant to do it.

Military Revolution: Musketeers, Artillery, and the Standing Army

Every ruler who centralizes a state has, at some point, to answer the same question: who holds the guns? For ninety years the Safavid answer had been the Qizilbash. The red-capped tribal cavalry were superb horsemen, fanatically devoted to the shah as a Sufi master, and utterly impossible to control. They fought when they pleased, withdrew when offended, feuded among themselves, and could plunge the empire into civil war whenever a succession came open. Abbas decided to build a different army.

The instrument of that change was the ghulam system. The word means "slave," and the institution had Ottoman parallels in the janissaries: young men, usually Christian by birth, taken as captives or tribute from the Caucasus - Georgians, Circassians, Armenians - converted to Islam, educated at court, and bound personally to the shah. They had no tribal kin, no ancestral lands, and no loyalty except to the man who had raised them. By the 1610s there were perhaps fifteen thousand ghulams under arms, with hundreds more serving as provincial governors, palace officials, and royal stewards. They were the spine of the new state.

Around the ghulams Abbas built a true standing army of three professional corps. The qurchi, the household cavalry, was expanded to roughly ten thousand men, drawn increasingly from selected Qizilbash but paid directly from the royal treasury rather than from tribal allotments. The tufangchi, a corps of musketeers numbering some twelve thousand, was something genuinely new in Iran - infantrymen recruited from the Persian peasantry, trained in firearms, and salaried by the crown. The topchi, the artillery corps, gave the shah for the first time a serious park of cannon, perhaps five hundred guns, complete with founders, gunners, and engineers.

The technical assistance came partly from Europe. In 1598 two English brothers, Anthony and Robert Shirley, arrived at Isfahan with a small entourage of gunners and metalworkers. Robert Shirley stayed for years, marrying a Circassian noblewoman, advising on artillery casting and infantry drill, and eventually serving as a Safavid ambassador to the courts of Europe. The Shirleys' role has sometimes been exaggerated by their own boasting and by later English chroniclers - Iranian smiths had been working with firearms for decades - but their presence symbolized something real. Abbas was prepared to learn from anyone, Christian or Muslim, who could teach him to win battles.

Paying for all this required a second revolution, quieter than the first but just as consequential. Traditional Safavid practice had granted vast provinces as *tiyul*, a kind of tax assignment, to Qizilbash chieftains who maintained tribal levies in return. Abbas began converting these lands into *khassa*, royal domain administered directly by crown officials, with revenues flowing to the central treasury at Isfahan. Province by province - Gilan, Mazandaran, Yazd, Kerman, much of Fars - the tribal map was redrawn. By the end of the reign, the shah controlled the bulk of Iran's productive land, and with it the cash to pay his salaried troops.

The result was a military machine unlike anything the Safavids had fielded before. It was multi-ethnic by design: Caucasian ghulams, Persian musketeers, Turkmen cavalry, Armenian and European technicians. It was paid in coin, not in tribal honor. And it was loyal, in the first instance, not to a tribe or a region but to the man on the throne. The Qizilbash were not destroyed - that would have been impossible and unwise - but they were now one component in a balanced system rather than its dominant force. When Abbas turned at last to face his external enemies, he did so with an army that no previous shah had ever commanded.

Recovering the East: Defeating the Uzbeks

He went east first. The Uzbeks under Abdullah Khan II had taken Herat in 1588 and Mashhad - the holiest Shia city in eastern Iran, home to the shrine of Imam Reza - in the same season. Uzbek troops were said to have stripped the gold from the dome and slaughtered worshippers. The desecration was a wound that every Iranian Shia felt personally. Abbas had been too weak to respond at his accession. He was not weak now.

The opportunity came when Abdullah Khan died in 1598 and the Uzbek confederation fractured into the usual succession wars. Abbas mobilized at once. That summer he marched into Khorasan with his new army - musketeers, artillery, ghulam cavalry - and at the battle of Rabat-i Pariyan, near Herat, he broke the Uzbek host. Mashhad was retaken. Herat followed. By the end of the year the entire province of Khorasan was once again Safavid, and the shah personally walked the last leagues to the shrine of Imam Reza as a barefoot pilgrim, an act of public penance and propaganda combined.

The eastern campaigns continued, in fits and starts, for years. Balkh was raided. Marv changed hands. The frontier was pushed back to roughly its old line along the Oxus and the Hindu Kush foothills. Beyond that, the desert and steppe defeated logistics on both sides; Abbas was realist enough to know that occupying Bukhara permanently was beyond his reach. What he wanted was security, and security he achieved. For the rest of his reign the eastern frontier remained quiet, the Uzbeks reduced to occasional raiders rather than existential threats.

The eastern victory mattered for reasons beyond the territory recovered. It validated the new army before any conservative critic could argue it had not been worth the upheaval. It restored Mashhad to

Safavid hands, allowing Abbas to lavish patronage on the shrine and to position himself as the protector of Twelver Shiism. It rebalanced the empire away from its old northwestern, Tabriz-centered orientation and toward a wider, more genuinely Iranian geography that included Khorasan, Fars, and the Persian Gulf. And it gave the shah, now in his early thirties, the prestige he needed to turn west.

There was also a quieter dividend. Among the populations resettled during these eastern campaigns were thousands of Khorasani families relocated to repopulate war-damaged regions, and tribesmen moved out of strategically sensitive areas. Abbas had discovered, or perhaps inherited, the habit of treating populations as instruments of policy - a habit he would soon employ on a much larger and more controversial scale in the Caucasus.

Recovering the West: Driving Out the Ottomans

The Treaty of Istanbul of 1590 had been a humiliation Abbas accepted because he had no choice. By 1603 he had a choice. The Ottomans were exhausted by a long war with the Habsburgs in Hungary and by the Celali rebellions tearing through Anatolia. Janissary mutinies had paralyzed Istanbul. Sultan Mehmed III had died young; his successor Ahmed I was a boy of thirteen. The eastern Ottoman frontier was held by garrisons that had not been paid in months.

Abbas struck in September 1603. The campaign was meticulously prepared and brilliantly executed. Tabriz fell after a short siege in October - the city that had been the original Safavid capital, lost for fourteen years, returned to Iranian hands in a matter of weeks. From Tabriz the army moved into Nakhchivan and Yerevan. Yerevan held out longer, its Ottoman garrison fighting through the winter, but it surrendered in June 1604. By the end of 1605 the entire region from the Aras River north into Georgia was once again Safavid.

The Ottoman counterattack came at Sufiyan, north of Tabriz, in November 1605. A large Ottoman army under the grand vizier Cigalazade Sinan Pasha advanced to retake the city. Abbas met him with a force perhaps half the size but far better led. The battle was a slaughter. The new Safavid artillery, deployed on a low ridge, broke the Ottoman cavalry charges; the ghulam horse and Qizilbash lancers then completed the encirclement. Cigalazade fled. Of an Ottoman army said to number a hundred thousand, perhaps a fifth survived. Sufiyan was the moment the Safavid military reforms paid their dividend in full.

The war dragged on for another seven years, but the strategic result was settled. The Treaty of Nasuh Pasha in 1612 confirmed the recovery of Tabriz, Shirvan, Georgia, Kurdistan, and Luristan - effectively undoing every Ottoman gain since the 1570s. A second round of fighting from 1623 to 1639 produced still greater triumphs. In 1623 Abbas marched into Iraq and took Baghdad itself, holding the city for fifteen years. With Baghdad came the Shia shrine cities of Najaf and Karbala - the tombs of Ali and Husayn, the holiest sites in Twelver Shiism. For a Safavid shah, this was symbolic conquest of the highest order.

Alongside the wars came the policy of forced relocation that would haunt Safavid memory for centuries. To deny resources to advancing Ottoman armies, Abbas ordered scorched-earth withdrawals across the Armenian highlands. Whole towns were emptied. The most famous case was Julfa, the prosperous Armenian merchant city on the Aras, whose population - perhaps twenty thousand - was marched south in 1604 to be resettled in a new suburb of Isfahan called New Julfa. Many died on the road. Those who survived became, by royal design, the silk-trading bourgeoisie of the Safavid economy, with global commercial networks reaching to Venice, Amsterdam, and Manila. Abbas had ruined them and made them rich in the same stroke. It was characteristic of the man.

In the south, meanwhile, he turned his attention to the Persian Gulf. The Portuguese had held the island of Hormuz at the mouth of the Gulf since 1507, controlling the maritime trade of the region and collecting tolls on every passing vessel. In 1622, in alliance with the English East India Company, Abbas's forces took Hormuz by combined siege and naval assault. The Portuguese were expelled. A new port, Bandar Abbas - "the harbor of Abbas" - was founded on the mainland opposite. For the first time in over a century, Iranian rulers controlled their own coast.

The Shah's Personality: Genius and Paranoia

European visitors to Isfahan in the 1610s and 1620s left vivid portraits of the man who had achieved all this. He was small and wiry, with a sharp face, a thick mustache, and dark restless eyes. He dressed plainly. He drank prodigiously. He spoke directly, often crudely, joked with his court, and could be charming to foreign envoys whom he wished to impress. He walked the bazaars of Isfahan in disguise to test the honesty of merchants, executing those who gave short measure. He prayed at Shia shrines with public ostentation and laughed at religious scholars in private. He spoke Turkish with his soldiers, Persian with his administrators, and a smattering of Arabic with his clerics. He was endlessly curious about Europe, India, and China, and listened carefully to anyone, of any rank, who could tell him something he did not know.

He worked harder than any of his predecessors. He read his own dispatches, dictated his own replies, traveled constantly between his provinces, and seemed to require less sleep than his secretaries. His memory for names and grievances was extraordinary. So was his memory for slights.

That last quality darkened with the years. Abbas had grown up in a court where princes routinely murdered their relatives to secure the throne, and where his own grandfather Tahmasp had blinded his brothers. He never forgot that the Qizilbash had killed his mother and brother, and he never quite trusted that they would not, given the chance, do the same to him or his sons. As he aged, the suspicion metastasized.

In 1615 he ordered the execution of his eldest son and heir, Safi Mirza. The young prince, a popular and capable commander, had perhaps spoken too freely; perhaps a courtier had whispered the wrong thing; perhaps Abbas, in a paranoid moment after a hunting trip, simply convinced himself that his son was plotting against him. The killing was carried out by a ghulam assassin. Abbas regretted it almost immediately, and contemporaries said he never fully recovered. Some chronicles describe him weeping at his son's tomb for years afterward.

Two other sons were blinded - the standard Safavid method of removing a prince from the line of succession without quite murdering him - on suspicion of conspiracy. By the time Abbas died in 1629, he had eliminated every viable adult heir. The throne passed to his grandson Sam Mirza, a sheltered seventeen-year-old who took the regnal name Safi and who had been raised, by his grandfather's order, in the harem rather than in the field. The institution of the harem-bred shah, isolated from administration and from the army, dates from this decision. It would prove, in time, the slow poison of the dynasty.

The contradiction sat at the heart of the man. The same calculating intelligence that built the ghulam corps and broke the Ottomans at Sufiyan also produced the orders that killed his own children. The same shah who founded New Julfa and welcomed European merchants ordered Armenian villages burned and their populations marched into exile. Abbas's biographers, Iranian and foreign, have struggled with him for four centuries because he refuses to settle into a single moral shape. He was, perhaps, simply a man who learned in adolescence that survival required absolute control, and who never afterward could imagine a life in which he might safely loosen his grip.

Analysis

The reign of Abbas I was the second founding of the Safavid Empire. Ismail had created the state in 1501 by riding a wave of tribal-religious enthusiasm; Abbas refounded it on the very different basis of bureaucratic centralization, salaried armies, royal monopolies, and a multi-ethnic ghulam elite. The first Safavid revolution had been Turkmen and charismatic. The second was Persian and administrative.

His achievements were genuine and durable. Abbas left an empire larger, richer, and safer than the one he had inherited. He left a capital, Isfahan, that within a generation would astonish European travelers as one of the most beautiful cities on earth. He left an economy integrated into global trade through Bandar Abbas and New Julfa. He left a confessional identity - Twelver Shiism, anchored at Mashhad, Najaf, and Karbala - that has shaped Iran ever since.

But he also left structural problems that his successors lacked the talent to solve. The destruction of Qizilbash autonomy removed a check on royal power, but it also removed a school of military leadership. The harem upbringing of his successors produced shahs who knew nothing of war or administration. Converting tribal lands to royal domain enriched the central treasury but eroded the local military aristocracy that had once defended the frontiers without instruction from Isfahan. The system worked brilliantly when a genius sat on the throne. It would not when one did not.

Quick Summary

- Abbas I came to power in 1588 at sixteen, executed his Qizilbash patron Murshid Quli Khan in 1589, and ruled until 1629.

- He bought peace with the Ottomans in 1590 to focus on internal reform, ceding Tabriz and the northwestern provinces temporarily.

- He built a standing army of ghulam slave-soldiers, salaried musketeers (tufangchi), and a modern artillery corps (topchi), aided by English advisors including Robert Shirley.

- He converted tribal lands to royal domain (khassa), funding the new army and centralizing power in Isfahan, his new capital from 1590.

- He defeated the Uzbeks in 1598, recovering Khorasan and the shrine of Mashhad.

- He defeated the Ottomans at Sufiyan in 1605, recovered Tabriz and the Caucasus, and took Baghdad in 1623.

- He expelled the Portuguese from Hormuz in 1622 with English help and founded Bandar Abbas.

- His paranoia led him to execute one son and blind two others, leaving the throne to an inexperienced grandson and weakening future succession.

When Abbas died in January 1629, after forty-one years on the throne, the Safavid Empire stood at the height of its power. No neighbor could threaten its frontiers. Its capital was a wonder. Its commerce reached three continents. Yet the very mechanisms that had produced this greatness - the centralized army, the harem-raised princes, the dependence on a single brilliant will at the center - carried the seeds of the dynasty's eventual decay. For the moment, none of that was visible. What was visible, to anyone who walked into the great square at Isfahan, was something that looked very much like the work of a king who had remade the world.

A remade army, a refilled treasury, a map redrawn in Iran's favor: these were the measurable achievements of Abbas's reign. But what a visitor to the empire in its prime actually saw, and what travelers carried home in their letters, was something harder to tabulate. It was a city. Abbas had moved his capital to Isfahan early in his reign and then spent three decades turning it into an argument in stone and tile: an argument about what Iranian kingship was, what Shi'a piety looked like at full volume, what commerce and ceremony could become when a single will arranged them around a single square.

Chapter 9:

Isfahan, Half the World

Twenty acres of open ground, ringed on four sides by a mosque, a palace, a shrine, and the mouth of a bazaar that funneled the commerce of three continents into a single plaza. Polo balls clacked across its length. Caravans unloaded silk from Gilan and indigo from Hindustan. On summer evenings, the shah himself watched from a balcony as cavalry wheeled below. The Persians coined a rhyme for what Abbas had built: *Isfahan nesf-e jahan* - Isfahan is half the world.

The square at the heart of that boast - Maydan-e Naqsh-e Jahan, the Image of the World - was not merely decoration. It was an argument in stone and tile. Shah Abbas the Great, who moved his capital there in 1598, wanted a city that announced Safavid Iran as the equal of Istanbul, Agra, and the courts of Christendom. He wanted a stage on which religion, commerce, kingship, and leisure could be performed simultaneously, within sight of one another. And he wanted it all arranged according to a single coherent design, laid out by royal command on what had been orchards and empty ground. Over three decades of patient construction, he got it. The result shaped Iranian urbanism for centuries and remains, four hundred years on, one of the largest public squares on earth.

Why Move the Capital?

Qazvin, the previous Safavid capital, had been chosen for defensive reasons. Tahmasp I moved the court there from Tabriz in the 1540s after Ottoman armies made the northwestern frontier untenable. For half a century it served the dynasty adequately. But by the time Abbas came to the throne in 1588, Qazvin's weaknesses had become glaring.

It sat too close to the Ottoman border. A hard campaigning season could put Turkish cavalry in its suburbs. It was cramped, its water supply uncertain, its position in the extreme northwest of a sprawling empire increasingly awkward as Abbas pushed Safavid power east toward Khorasan and south toward the Persian Gulf. A capital on the geographic periphery could not easily coordinate a realm that stretched from the Tigris to the Oxus.

Isfahan answered every one of these problems. It lay in the center of the Iranian plateau, at roughly equal distance from the empire's frontiers. The Zayandeh Rud - the life-giving river - watered orchards and rice paddies in abundance, supporting a large urban population without the Achilles heel of a single aqueduct. The city sat astride the main north-south caravan roads and within reach of the Gulf ports where Abbas was busy cultivating European merchants. It had been a major city since Seljuk times, with a grand congregational mosque and an established merchant class. And it was far enough from the Ottoman frontier that no sudden raid could threaten the throne.

There was also a political logic. A new capital meant a fresh slate. Qazvin was thick with the old Qizilbash aristocracy, the Turkmen tribal commanders whose power Abbas was systematically trimming. By relocating his court to Isfahan and building, in effect, a new imperial quarter on open ground south of the old city, Abbas could surround himself with a bureaucracy and a household of his own choosing - Georgian and Armenian ghulams, Persian administrators, loyal clerics - without the dead weight of factions that had dominated earlier reigns.

Moving a capital is never simply an administrative act. It is a declaration. Peter the Great would make the same kind of gesture a century later when he dragged Russia's center of gravity to a swamp on the Baltic. Abbas was doing something similar: severing the court from its tribal past, planting it in the Iranian heartland, and building around it a city that would proclaim the new order. In 1598 the royal household moved south. The construction crews had already begun.

Designing the Maydan

The square that took shape between 1598 and 1629 was roughly 560 meters long and 160 meters wide - seven times the size of Venice's Piazza San Marco, more than twice the size of Moscow's Red Square. By most measures it was the largest planned public space anywhere in the early modern world. And unlike most great squares, which accrete over centuries as different rulers add monuments, this one was conceived as a single composition.

The plan was simple and severe. A vast rectangle, oriented roughly north to south. Two stories of arcaded shops running continuously around its entire perimeter, so that the square presented an unbroken architectural frame. Four monumental portals, one at the midpoint of each side, each leading to a different institution: the Qeysarieh Bazaar to the north, the Royal Mosque to the south, the Sheikh Lotfollah Mosque to the east, and the Ali Qapu palace gate to the west. Each portal was a masterpiece in its own right, each oriented with mathematical deliberation to face its opposite across the open ground.

The geometry was not arbitrary. Four portals on four sides echoed the classical Persian *chahar bagh*, the fourfold garden of paradise, and the four-iwan plan of the great Iranian mosques. The square, in a sense, was a garden scaled up to the dimensions of statecraft - an earthly paradise whose walls enclosed not flowers but the core institutions of Safavid civilization: the market, the mosque, the royal shrine, and the palace.

Function followed form with uncommon flexibility. For most of the year the maydan was a commercial space, its arcaded shops selling textiles, ceramics, ironwork, spices, and carpets. On festival days it converted into a theater of state. Chroniclers describe polo matches played along its length, with stone goalposts that still stand at the north and south ends. They describe military reviews in which Abbas displayed his new standing army - the *tofangchis* with their muskets, the cavalry in chain mail, the artillery trains purchased through English intermediaries. They describe fireworks, wrestling matches, public executions, and the reception of foreign ambassadors who were made to cross the vast space on foot so that by the time they reached the throne they had already been impressed into humility.

The European visitors were. Pietro della Valle, Thomas Herbert, the Sherley brothers, Jean Chardin, Adam Olearius - each in turn recorded their astonishment. Chardin, the Huguenot jeweler who spent years at the Safavid court in the 1660s and 1670s, called the maydan the noblest plaza he had ever seen, and Chardin had seen Rome. He counted the shops. He described the water channels that ran along the edges, fed from the Zayandeh Rud, cooling the air and watering the plane trees. He noted the bronze cannon captured from the Portuguese at Hormuz, displayed near the southern gate as trophies.

What no visitor could miss was the simultaneity of the place. Stand in the middle of the square on a busy afternoon and you saw, in a single glance, the pillars of Safavid life coexisting. Merchants haggled under one arcade. Clerics filed into the mosque under another. The shah's balcony loomed to the west. The private royal chapel, its dome shimmering, closed off the east. Commerce, faith, kingship, and devotion - all within earshot of one another, all framed by the same arcade. No earlier Iranian city had been composed in quite this way. Abbas had built not just a plaza but a diagram of his empire.

The Royal Mosque and the Sheikh Lotfollah

Two mosques anchored the maydan, and they could not have been more different in purpose or effect.

At the southern end rose the Masjed-e Shah, the Royal Mosque, begun in 1611 and not finished until after Abbas's death. Built on a scale intended to rival the great Seljuk monuments of the old city, its entrance portal on the maydan was a cliff of turquoise tilework, thirty meters high, crowned by honeycombed muqarnas that dissolved the transition between wall and vault into a cascade of painted stalactites.

Behind the portal the mosque pivoted some forty-five degrees - a structural sleight of hand demanded by the fact that the square was oriented to the cardinal directions while Mecca lay to the southwest. Worshippers entered facing one way and emerged, through a short vestibule, oriented correctly toward the qibla.

Inside, the Royal Mosque deployed every trick in the Persian architectural repertoire. A vast central courtyard with four iwans. A sanctuary covered by a double dome that rose fifty-three meters and echoed with a famous acoustic - a clap beneath its apex returns seven times. Tilework in cuerda seca, a technique of outlining colors with a greasy black line that allowed faster production than the older mosaic faience, covering every surface in arabesques, inscriptions, and floral medallions. It was built for crowds, built to shelter the congregational Friday prayer of an entire capital. It was, unmistakably, a public building.

The Sheikh Lotfollah Mosque, directly across the square on the eastern side, was the opposite. Small, with no minarets and no courtyard, it did not gather worshippers in large numbers, and there was no public entrance for the faithful at all. The chief architect, Muhammad Reza, began work in 1603 under Abbas's direct patronage; the mosque was completed in 1619.

A private royal chapel named for a revered Lebanese Shi'a scholar whom Abbas had invited to Isfahan as a teacher, the Sheikh Lotfollah was distinguished above all by its dome - low, broad, tiled not in the standard turquoise but in a pale café-au-lait ground scattered with dark blue arabesques that shifted hue through the day. It stands as one of the most subtle and perfect enclosures in the history of Islamic architecture. A bent corridor, hidden beneath the maydan, connected the mosque directly to the Ali Qapu palace opposite. The shah and the women of his household could cross from residence to devotion without ever appearing in public.

Inside, the effect was of a jewel box. The dome's interior was covered in tile medallions arranged in concentric rings of descending peacock-feather patterns, the whole composition organized around a central sunburst that, when struck by sunlight through the high grilled windows, flared into gold. There were no columns. The space was unified, silent, intimate. Where the Royal Mosque overwhelmed with scale, the Sheikh Lotfollah seduced with proportion.

The dialogue between the two mosques across the maydan was not accidental. One addressed the community, the other the dynasty. One was the mosque of the shah as sovereign of the faithful; the other of the shah as a private Shi'a believer. That both could stand within sight of each other, executed by the same workshops in the same decade, suggested a state confident enough to separate its public and private faces - and wealthy enough to lavish on each the finest craftsmanship its workshops could produce. The Sheikh Lotfollah would be lovingly restored in the 1920s under Reza Shah, but most of what the modern visitor sees is the original work of Muhammad Reza and his teams.

Ali Qapu and the Chehel Sotun: A Persian Versailles

On the western side of the square stood the Ali Qapu, the High Gate, the ceremonial portal of the royal palace complex that extended westward behind it into gardens and pavilions. The name borrowed Ottoman vocabulary - the Sublime Porte at Istanbul was the *Bab-e Ali* - but the building itself was distinctly Persian. Six stories tall, topped by a deep covered veranda whose slender wooden columns supported a flat roof, the Ali Qapu served as Shah Abbas's grandstand. From its talar he reviewed parades, watched polo, received ambassadors, and observed the public life of the square below while remaining elevated, framed, and partially withdrawn.

The building's interior rooms were small in comparison to its commanding exterior. Decorated with painted stucco, gilded niches, and - most famously - a music room on the upper floor whose walls were carved into vessel-shaped recesses, they rewarded close attention.

The niches served a double function: they displayed the shah's collection of porcelain and glass, and they improved the acoustics of chamber music played for the royal household. Behind painted flowers and Chinese-inspired dragons, the court listened to the lutes and drums of Safavid musicians in a space engineered to flatter every note.

Behind the Ali Qapu extended the *dowlatkhaneh*, the royal precinct, a planned sequence of gardens, canals, and pavilions stretching nearly to the river. Under Abbas and his successors, a distinctly Safavid style of palace building flowered in these gardens. Unlike the massive enclosed palaces of European monarchs, Safavid royal architecture favored the *kushk*, the garden pavilion - small in footprint, open on at least one side to a reflecting pool, set within geometrically arranged plantings of plane trees, cypresses, and flowering shrubs.

The masterpiece of the type was the Chehel Sotun, the Palace of Forty Columns, built under Shah Abbas II in the mid-seventeenth century. Its name was a poetic conceit: the pavilion had twenty slender wooden columns supporting its great talar; the other twenty were the reflections thrown back by the long pool in front of it. Inside, the walls were painted with enormous historical frescoes - battles, receptions, courtly banquets, scenes of Abbas the Great welcoming Mughal princes and Uzbek khans. These were among the largest figural paintings ever produced in Safavid Iran, a reminder that the prohibition on representational art in religious contexts did not extend to secular palaces.

European visitors, groping for comparisons, sometimes called Isfahan a Persian Versailles. The analogy captures the ambition but misses the aesthetic. Versailles was about enclosure, hierarchy, and the compression of the state into a single monumental building. Safavid palace design was about dispersal - a necklace of pavilions scattered through gardens, each a small perfection, linked by water channels and avenues. Power in the Safavid conception was not concentrated in a single façade. It radiated outward through a series of carefully composed spaces.

And it radiated downward. The gardens behind the Ali Qapu were not exclusively royal. On certain festival days they were opened to the public, and the Chahar Bagh avenue - the great tree-lined boulevard that Abbas drove south from the precinct to the river - was designed from the outset as a promenade where townspeople could walk, picnic, and be seen. This was a different theory of monarchy from the one developing in contemporary France. The shah displayed himself to his people; he did not hide from them.

Bridges, Gardens, and the Zayandeh Rud

No account of Abbas's Isfahan makes sense without the river. The Zayandeh Rud, the life-giver, ran east-west across the southern edge of the city, fed by snowmelt from the Zagros and disappearing into a salt marsh a hundred miles to the east. Not large by the standards of the great rivers of Asia - in late summer it dwindled to a trickle - it was nonetheless everything to Isfahan, watering the orchards and rice fields that fed the capital and providing the one element without which no Persian city could flourish: flowing water in abundance.

Abbas made the river central to his urban plan. The Chahar Bagh avenue, lined with a central water channel and four rows of plane trees, ran from the royal precinct down to the riverbank and continued on the far side through the new suburb of Julfa, where Abbas had resettled thousands of Armenian merchants from the Caucasus to manage the silk trade. To link the two halves of the city he built a bridge that was also a dam, a promenade, and a monument.

The Allahverdi Khan Bridge, better known as the Si-o-se Pol, the Bridge of Thirty-Three Arches, stretched nearly three hundred meters across the riverbed. It had two tiers of arcaded walkways, teahouses built into its piers, and was wide enough for caravans to pass. Downstream, the later Khaju Bridge combined its function as a river crossing with that of a weir, raising the water level for irrigation and providing stepped platforms where the public could sit and watch the river flow beneath. These bridges were not utilitarian afterthoughts.

They were civic architecture of a very high order, as carefully composed as the mosques on the maydan.

Gardens threaded the entire composition. Safavid gardens followed the chahar bagh plan - fourfold, divided by water channels representing the four rivers of paradise described in the Qur'an - but at Isfahan they were scaled up and linked into networks. The Hasht Behesht, the Eight Paradises pavilion, sat at the heart of a royal garden north of the river. The Bagh-e Naqsh-e Jahan, the garden from which the great square took its name, had been the nucleus around which Abbas laid out his new capital. Water flowed from the river up through channels into each of these gardens, cooling the pavilions, sustaining the plantings, and turning the city, in the words of one European traveler, into a single vast green carpet unfolded on the plateau.

The Armenian quarter at New Julfa deserves mention of its own. Abbas deported the Armenians of Old Julfa from their home city on the Aras in 1604 - a brutal act, dressed up as resettlement - but then invested heavily in their new quarter south of the river. They were granted religious autonomy, permission to build churches, and effective monopolies on parts of the silk trade. By the 1620s Julfa had become one of the great commercial hubs of Eurasia, with Armenian firms operating networks that reached from Amsterdam to Manila. Much of the capital's international commerce flowed through their hands.

Key Figures & Events

Shah Abbas the Great conceived the project and drove it forward for three decades, personally overseeing the architectural decisions and the recruitment of craftsmen. Muhammad Reza designed and built the Sheikh Lotfollah Mosque between 1603 and 1619, producing in the process one of the most refined domes in the history of Islamic architecture. Allahverdi Khan, the Georgian ghulam general who rose to become Abbas's most trusted commander, lent his name and his patronage to the Si-o-se Pol bridge. Sheikh Lotfollah al-Amili, the

Lebanese Shi'a scholar for whom the royal chapel was named, represented the wave of Arab clerics Abbas imported to consolidate Twelver doctrine in his capital. Chardin, Olearius, Della Valle, Thomas Herbert, and other European travelers recorded what they saw and carried the legend of Isfahan westward through their published accounts.

Analysis

What did Abbas accomplish by building Isfahan? On one level, a feat of urbanism. He took a provincial city of perhaps 80,000 and, within a generation, expanded it into a capital of perhaps half a million - one of the largest cities in the world around 1630, rivaling London and Paris in population and arguably surpassing them in planned magnificence.

On a deeper level he accomplished something more enduring. He crystallized a Safavid imperial identity in built form. The four portals of the maydan - bazaar, royal mosque, royal chapel, palace - were not a random collection of buildings. They were a statement about what the Safavid state was: a Shi'a monarchy resting on four pillars of commerce, public religion, dynastic piety, and kingship. By placing them in visual dialogue around a single open space, Abbas made that theory of the state legible to anyone who walked through his capital.

He also demonstrated that Iran could be, once again, a cultural center of the first rank. The craftsmen who tiled the Royal Mosque and painted the walls of the Chehel Sotun were heirs to a tradition that stretched back through the Timurid ateliers of Herat to the Ilkhanid workshops of Tabriz. Under Abbas's patronage that tradition produced some of its highest achievements. The fact that the results still stand - that UNESCO designated the maydan a World Heritage Site in 1979, that the Sheikh Lotfollah still dazzles, that the bridges still carry evening strollers above the river - testifies to how well they were made.

The boast was not idle. Isfahan, in the half-century after Abbas laid it out, really did function as half the world: a crossroads through which the commerce, diplomacy, and religious currents of Asia and Europe passed, and which each of them took the measure of in turn.

Quick Summary

- In 1598 Shah Abbas moved the Safavid capital from Qazvin to Isfahan for strategic, logistical, and political reasons.

- Naqsh-e Jahan Square, built between 1598 and 1629, measured roughly 560 by 160 meters and was framed by a continuous two-story arcade with four monumental portals.

- The Royal Mosque (Masjed-e Shah), the large congregational mosque at the southern end, pivoted forty-five degrees to align with Mecca and featured legendary acoustics beneath its double dome.

- The Sheikh Lotfollah Mosque, built by Muhammad Reza between 1603 and 1619 on the eastern side, served as a private royal chapel, connected by a tunnel to the palace opposite.

- The Ali Qapu palace on the western side included a celebrated music room; its gardens extended westward into a complex of pavilions including the later Chehel Sotun.

- The Zayandeh Rud river defined the southern edge of the city, crossed by the Si-o-se Pol and Khaju bridges, both masterpieces of public architecture.

- The Armenian suburb of New Julfa, founded by forced resettlement in 1604, became a hub of global commerce.

- The maydan and its monuments were designated a UNESCO World Heritage Site in 1979.

Four centuries after Shah Abbas laid his plumb lines across the orchards south of Isfahan, the square he built remains substantially as he conceived it - a rare fate for an early modern capital. Cities like Delhi, Istanbul, and Paris have been repeatedly rebuilt; their early modern monuments survive as islands in a changed sea. Isfahan's maydan survives as a complete composition, still framed by its arcade, still anchored by its four portals, still functioning as a market and a place of public gathering. To stand at its center at sunset, as the tile of the domes shifts from turquoise to indigo and the call to prayer rises from the Royal Mosque, is to understand why an Englishman called it the noblest plaza he had ever seen - and why a Persian poet, looking for a phrase worthy of it, reached past comparison and settled for half the world.

A square framed by a mosque, a palace, a shrine, and a bazaar was not an accidental composition. The bazaar belonged there because the empire Abbas built could not be understood apart from the commerce that flowed through it. The tile and the caravan were parts of a single system. Silk from Gilan, indigo from Hindustan, silver from Potosí: the wealth that raised the domes of Isfahan arrived along routes that stretched from the Caspian villages to the looms of Lyon. To see the Safavid achievement whole, one has to follow the bales out of the maydan and onto the roads.

Chapter 10:

Silk, Silver, and the World Economy

In the 1620s, a bale of raw silk spun from cocoons in the hills of Gilan might leave a Caspian village on the back of a mule, cross the Iranian plateau in a caravan of a thousand animals, transfer at Isfahan to an Armenian factor with relatives in Venice and Amsterdam, sail down the Persian Gulf under an English flag, round the Cape of Good Hope in a Dutch hull, and end its journey on a loom in Lyon. Somewhere along the way, it would be paid for in silver mined by forced labor in Potosí.

The Safavid Empire was not a hermit kingdom of turbaned mystics. It was one of the critical hinges of the first genuinely global economy, a realm whose fortunes rose and fell with decisions taken in London boardrooms and Mexican mineshafts. Under Shah Abbas I and his successors, Iran became a vast clearinghouse where raw silk from the Caspian provinces was exchanged for New World bullion, Indian indigo, English broadcloth, and Chinese porcelain. The state tried to control this trade; foreign companies tried to capture it; and an Armenian merchant class, resettled by royal decree into a single suburb of Isfahan, outmaneuvered both. Understanding how silk and silver moved through Safavid Iran is the best way to grasp why the empire grew so rich in the seventeenth century - and why that wealth proved so difficult to defend.

The Silk Monopoly and Royal Trade

Silk was Iran's oil. The mulberry groves of Gilan, Mazandaran, and Shirvan along the Caspian coast produced a raw silk that European weavers prized above almost any other. By the late sixteenth century, Iranian silk clothed the backs of Polish nobles, Venetian senators, and eventually the burghers of Amsterdam. Whoever controlled its export controlled one of the most lucrative commodity streams on the planet.

Shah Abbas I grasped this with a clarity that few early modern rulers could match. Beginning around 1619, he moved to transform silk from a private trade into a royal monopoly. Merchants who wished to buy raw silk were required, in principle, to purchase it directly from the crown or from state-licensed intermediaries. Those who tried to operate outside the system faced punishing taxes. The shah was, in effect, turning himself into the largest single silk broker in Eurasia.

The motive was partly fiscal and partly strategic. Abbas needed hard currency to pay his new standing army of *ghulams* and to finance the building of Isfahan. He also wanted to starve the Ottomans, through whose territory silk had traditionally flowed to Aleppo and Bursa, of the customs revenue they had long milked from the trade. Rerouting Iranian silk southward to the Persian Gulf and onto European ships would simultaneously fill his own treasury and drain his rival's.

To make the monopoly work, Abbas relied on a cadre of royal merchants - many of them Armenian - who bought silk on the crown's behalf, stored it in royal warehouses, and negotiated its sale to foreign buyers. Caravans moving silk between Gilan and Isfahan traveled under state protection. Accounts kept by European factors describe wagonloads of raw silk arriving at the capital to be auctioned off, with the shah's agents setting floor prices and taking their cut.

It never worked as cleanly as the decree suggested. Smuggling through Ottoman territory continued. Local governors in the Caspian provinces skimmed supplies for private sale. Ambassadors sent from Europe complained bitterly that promised deliveries arrived late, short, or adulterated with inferior grades. A royal monopoly in a realm the size of Iran was less an iron grip than an elaborate negotiation, constantly renegotiated with every provincial khan and village headman in the silk belt.

After Abbas I's death in 1629, his successors loosened the formal monopoly, but the pattern he had established endured. Royal merchants - men who held court appointments and enjoyed privileged access to the silk supply - continued to dominate the trade well into the second half of the seventeenth century. The crown remained the single most important player in the market, even when it was no longer the only legal one.

The results, for a time, were spectacular. Customs revenues at the Gulf ports surged. European silver poured into Iranian mints. Isfahan, which a generation earlier had been a provincial town, blossomed into a capital whose covered bazaars stocked Venetian glass, Chinese silk, and Indian diamonds. The silk monopoly was the engine that financed the Safavid golden age.

New Julfa and the Armenian Diaspora

Walk south across the Zayandeh River from the center of old Isfahan and you enter a different city. The streets are narrower, the church bells - still ringing, four centuries later - carry a different cadence, and the houses bear the unmistakable stamp of Armenian craftsmanship. This is New Julfa, the suburb that Shah Abbas I carved out in 1605 for a population he had forcibly transplanted from the Armenian town of Julfa on the Aras River, then under threat of Ottoman invasion.

The deportation was brutal. Contemporaries describe columns of Armenian families driven south across the Iranian plateau, with thousands dying of hunger and exhaustion along the way. The survivors, resettled in a purpose-built quarter of the capital, received something unusual for a refugee population: an effective charter of self-government, the right to practice Christianity openly, tax privileges, and - most consequentially - a royal license to handle the silk trade.

Abbas had chosen them deliberately. The Armenians of old Julfa had been merchants for generations, with branch houses across the

Ottoman Empire, in Mughal India, and as far north as Muscovy. They spoke Persian, Turkish, Italian, and Russian. They knew how to price silk in Aleppo and bullion in Venice. They possessed the one asset the shah could not manufacture: a working diaspora.

From New Julfa, the Armenian trading network expanded with astonishing speed. Family firms dispatched younger sons to establish offices in Aleppo, Izmir, Venice, Livorno, Marseille, Amsterdam, London, Moscow, Astrakhan, Lhasa, Manila, and Madras. A letter written from Isfahan in Armenian could reach a cousin in Cadiz within a few months, carrying instructions on prices, exchange rates, and the creditworthiness of particular buyers. Records preserved in the archives of the Mxit'arist congregation in Venice, and in the account books of individual firms such as the house of Minasian, reveal a commercial infrastructure that rivaled anything the European chartered companies could muster.

What made the New Julfa system work was trust. These were men who lent to one another across continents on the strength of a signed bill of exchange, knowing that a default would ruin a family's standing in the close-knit society back home. Disputes were arbitrated by the *kalantar*, the hereditary mayor of the suburb, whose verdicts carried the force of both religious and communal sanction. It was a capitalism built not on impersonal contract law but on reputation, kinship, and the memory of who had behaved honorably in Aleppo forty years before.

By the mid-seventeenth century, the New Julfans were probably the single largest private handler of Iranian silk exports. They carried Persian silk to Europe and returned with Spanish reals, Dutch guilders, and Italian cloth. They ran a parallel trade to the east, shipping silk and cash to India and bringing back textiles, indigo, and diamonds. A few of their grandest merchants lived in palaces decorated with Italianate frescoes and Safavid tilework, educated their daughters in French, and endowed cathedrals whose interiors still astonish visitors.

The New Julfans also performed a service that no one else could. When the Safavid treasury needed short-term credit, or when a European ambassador needed a discreet loan, it was often an Armenian merchant who advanced the funds. They were the bankers of a state that did not quite have banks. This made them indispensable - and, when the empire finally began to stagger in the 1720s, it also made them vulnerable, for wealth held by a minority community is always the easiest to confiscate.

The English and Dutch East India Companies in Persia

The Europeans who arrived in Safavid Iran in the early seventeenth century came not as conquerors but as supplicants. They represented chartered joint-stock companies - the English East India Company, founded in 1600, and the Dutch VOC, founded in 1602 - which had been empowered by their governments to trade in Asia. They needed silk. The shah had silk. The terms of exchange, both sides understood, would be set in Isfahan.

The English arrived first in serious numbers. In 1616, their factors began probing the Iranian market, and within a few years they had secured a royal firman permitting trade. The key figure in opening the door was Robert Sherley, an English adventurer who had entered Abbas's service in 1599 and become, improbably, a Safavid ambassador to the courts of Europe. Sherley's long lobbying persuaded both James I and Abbas that an Anglo-Iranian silk trade, bypassing the Ottomans, was in their mutual interest.

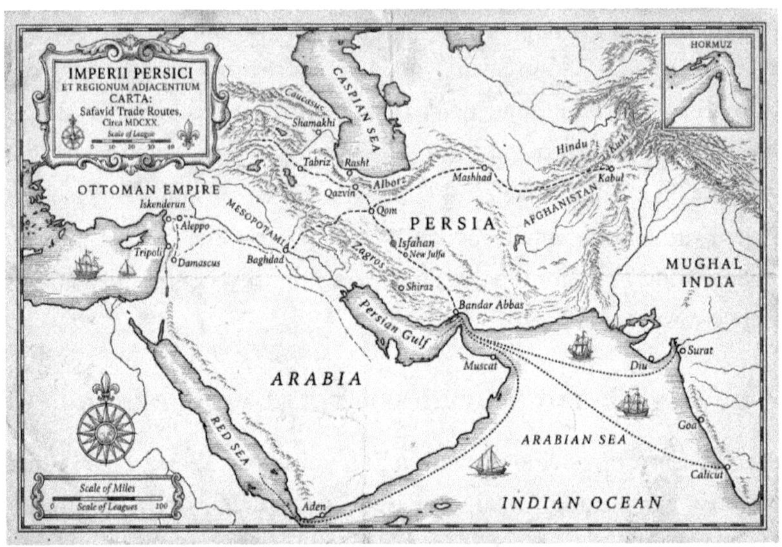

Safavid Trade Networks and the Silk Routes, c. 1620

The initial years were promising. English ships carried Iranian silk from the Gulf to London, where it was worked by weavers in Spitalfields and Canterbury. In return the Company shipped English broadcloth - a product for which, as it turned out, there was only limited Iranian demand - supplemented by large quantities of silver specie. The imbalance was uncomfortable: the English could never sell enough cloth to pay for the silk they wanted, and had to make up the difference in bullion shipped out of England, provoking mercantilist hand-wringing back home.

Sir Thomas Roe, the veteran ambassador who had served in Mughal India, was among the loudest skeptics. The Persian silk trade, he warned, was too risky, too expensive, and too dependent on the whims of a single ruler. The outbound voyage was long, the Gulf was dangerous, and the shah could alter the price of silk by royal decree. Roe's gloom proved prescient. By around 1640 the English silk trade into Iran was already contracting, and the Company's attention was shifting decisively toward India, where cotton textiles offered faster profits and fewer monopolistic headaches.

The Dutch proved more persistent and, for a while, more successful. The VOC opened a factory at Bandar Abbas in 1623 and steadily expanded its operations, eventually outstripping the English in volume. The Dutch had two advantages. Their Asian network was denser, which allowed them to pay for Iranian silk partly with spices, sugar, and Japanese silver funneled through Batavia - reducing their need to ship bullion from Europe. And they were more willing to play a long game, accepting thin margins on silk in exchange for the privilege of moving other goods through Iranian customs at preferential rates.

Neither company found Iran an easy market. The royal monopoly meant that prices were often set arbitrarily. Customs officials demanded gifts. Shipments were delayed by the seasonal rhythms of the caravans. European factors, stationed for years in Isfahan or Bandar Abbas, wrote home complaining of heat, dysentery, and the endless delicacy of court politics. Several drank themselves to death. A surprising number converted to Islam, married locally, and vanished from Company records.

What the Dutch and English eventually recognized was that, in Iran, they were junior partners in a trade dominated by the New Julfans. Armenian merchants routinely carried silk to Europe more cheaply and reliably than the companies could. The chartered corporations never broke that grip. By the end of the seventeenth century, the Dutch were still turning a profit at Bandar Abbas, but the Iranian trade had become a sideshow in a commercial empire now centered on Java and Bengal.

Bandar Abbas and the Loss of Hormuz

For nearly a century before Abbas I's reign, the Persian Gulf had been a Portuguese lake. Its key was the island fortress of Hormuz, seized by Afonso de Albuquerque in 1515, which commanded the strait through which all seaborne trade between the Gulf and the Indian Ocean had to pass. From Hormuz, the Portuguese extracted customs, convoyed pilgrims, and humiliated any Muslim ruler foolish enough to challenge them.

Shah Abbas resented this intensely, but he lacked a navy. What he had instead, after 1616, was the English East India Company, whose ships were already cruising the Gulf in search of a trading foothold. The bargain that followed was one of the neater pieces of diplomacy in the seventeenth century. In 1622, a combined Anglo-Iranian force - Iranian soldiers carried and supported by English warships - besieged Hormuz. The Portuguese garrison, undersupplied and outgunned, capitulated after a few weeks.

The shah got his strait. The English got their reward: a share of the customs receipts, trading privileges, and a permanent foothold at the mainland port just across from Hormuz. That port, previously a fishing village called Gamrun, was renamed Bandar Abbas - the Shah's Port. It would serve for the next century as the principal maritime gateway of the Safavid Empire.

Bandar Abbas was a strange, harsh place. Its summer heat was legendary; European factors spoke of retreating into cellars to survive the midday furnace. Drinking water had to be carried in from distant wells. Malaria was endemic. And yet the warehouses of the English, Dutch, and later the French stood side by side along the waterfront, crammed with silk bales waiting for the monsoon ships and with Indian textiles just unloaded.

The fall of Hormuz had consequences beyond the immediate redirection of trade. It signaled that the Portuguese century in the Indian Ocean was ending. It brought the Safavids, for the first time, into direct fiscal partnership with European chartered companies, whose customs payments became a substantial line in the imperial budget. And it embedded the Gulf ports in the emerging world economy: Bandar Abbas was where Iranian silk met Mexican silver, Dutch spices, and Indian cotton in a single bustling market.

The arrangement carried risks. Customs revenues depended on foreign shipping. When European traders quarreled with the court, the crown lost income. When piracy surged - as it did repeatedly in the later seventeenth century, with Omani Arab fleets raiding the Gulf - trade contracted and the port city suffered. By the early eighteenth century, Bandar Abbas was visibly declining, its population shrinking, its warehouses half-empty. The strategic coup of 1622 had paid handsome dividends for a century, but those dividends were not permanent.

Coinage, Caravanserais, and the Inland Trade

The seaborne trade captures the imagination, but most goods in Safavid Iran still moved by land. The great trunk roads - from Tabriz to Isfahan, from Isfahan to Shiraz and the Gulf, from Isfahan east to Mashhad and on to Central Asia - were lined with caravanserais, those squat fortified inns built at roughly a day's march apart. Many of them still stand. Step inside one today and you can still see the stables on the ground floor and the merchants' cells arranged along the upper gallery, the architecture of a commercial civilization that moved at the pace of a loaded camel.

Shah Abbas I invested heavily in this infrastructure. Royal endowments, or *waqfs*, funded the construction of caravanserais, bridges, and covered bazaars across the empire. The road network was policed, with varying effectiveness, by a corps of mounted guards. A traveling merchant could, in principle, expect lodging, fodder, and security every evening of a months-long journey. The fact that so many Armenian, Indian, and Jewish traders did in fact complete such journeys suggests the system, for all its imperfections, worked.

Into this network poured the silver of the New World. Spanish reals minted from Potosí bullion, arriving via Aleppo or via European ships at Bandar Abbas, were melted down in Iranian mints and reissued as *abbasis* and *shahis*, the silver coins bearing the shah's name. Studies of surviving Safavid coinage show how closely its silver content tracked the global bullion market: when New World mines slowed their output in the later seventeenth century, Iranian coins grew lighter and scarcer.

This monetary dependence was a vulnerability the Safavids never solved. Iran produced silk, carpets, and rosewater in abundance, but it mined little silver. Its coinage relied on imports, which meant that its money supply was hostage to forces beyond any shah's control. When the Gulf trade faltered in the 1690s and early 1700s, bullion inflows dropped, the mints slowed, prices rose, and tax revenues - collected largely in cash - began to fall behind the needs of the state.

The inland trade carried on regardless, quieter than the maritime story but no less essential. Indian merchants, especially Hindus from Multan, settled in Isfahan and the northern cities, running credit networks that financed the caravan trade between Iran and the subcontinent. Central Asian traders brought horses, slaves, and rhubarb. Ottoman merchants, despite official hostilities, kept the overland routes to Aleppo open. Beneath the grand narrative of competing empires, a dense commercial ecology hummed along, year after year, largely indifferent to who held the throne in Isfahan.

Analysis

The Safavid Empire's integration into the world economy was both its making and, eventually, part of its undoing. The silk trade, the Armenian diaspora, the European factories, and the silver-fed mints together produced a century of prosperity that financed the architectural glories of Isfahan, the standing army of the *ghulams*, and the charitable endowments that still shape Iranian cities. Abbas I's genius lay in recognizing that a landlocked empire could plug itself into global commerce by playing the great powers against one another and by harnessing a diaspora community that no rival possessed.

The system's vulnerabilities, though, were structural. It depended on foreign silver, foreign ships, and a trading class that, however indispensable, was religiously and ethnically distinct from the ruling majority. When the world economy shifted - when Bengali silk and Chinese tea outcompeted Iranian exports, when the European companies turned their energies to India, when bullion flows slowed -

the Safavid state lacked the fiscal tools to adjust. It had no central bank, no public debt, no mechanism to cushion a downturn. The prosperity had been real, but it had also been contingent, a function of flows that Isfahan did not control.

Quick Summary

- Shah Abbas I established a royal silk monopoly around 1619, making the crown the dominant broker of Iran's most valuable export.

- The forced resettlement of Armenians from old Julfa to New Julfa in 1605 created a diaspora trading network spanning Europe, the Middle East, and Asia.

- The English East India Company began trading in Iran in 1616 but withdrew from silk by around 1640; the Dutch VOC persisted longer and more profitably.

- The 1622 Anglo-Iranian capture of Hormuz ended Portuguese dominance of the Persian Gulf and established Bandar Abbas as Iran's main maritime port.

- Iranian coinage depended on imported New World silver, making the money supply vulnerable to global bullion flows.

- Royal investment in caravanserais and roads supported a vast inland trade involving Armenian, Indian, and Central Asian merchants.

- By the early 1700s, piracy, European competition, and slowing silver inflows were eroding the economic foundations of the empire.

For a century and a quarter, Isfahan was a genuine node of the global economy, a city where Dutch factors, Armenian financiers, Indian bankers, and Iranian officials negotiated the price of silk in half a dozen languages. That cosmopolitan prosperity left a physical legacy - the bridges, bazaars, churches, and mosques that still draw visitors - and a deeper one: the memory, embedded in Iranian historical consciousness, of a time when the country stood not at the periphery of world commerce but very near its center. When the Safavid system finally collapsed in the 1720s, it was not simply a dynasty that fell. An entire commercial order, painfully assembled over four generations, came apart with it.

An entire commercial order was assembled over four generations, and the silver it drew into Iran did not stay in the treasury. Much of it flowed into workshops where the empire conducted a different kind of trade, one whose currency was prestige rather than coin. If Safavid silk paid for Safavid power, Safavid painting, calligraphy, and carpet-weaving displayed it. The shahs who negotiated with Dutch factors and Armenian bankers were the same shahs who sat for hours with master illuminators, pricing a single manuscript page at the cost of a village. Wealth was one form of Safavid soft power. Beauty was the other.

Chapter 11:

The Brush and the Pen

In Safavid workshops, painters illuminated manuscripts that took decades to complete and sold for the price of a small army. Calligraphers were honored above generals. A single page by Reza Abbasi could become a courtier's most prized possession, wrapped in silk, traded like currency, studied like scripture.

Few societies have ever lavished so much wealth, talent, and bureaucratic attention on things made of paper, pigment, and wool. The Safavid shahs ran the most ambitious cultural workshop of the early modern world, a factory of beauty in which the boundary between political power and aesthetic refinement simply dissolved. A royal library, the *kitabkhana*, was not a quiet reading room but a vast atelier where designers, gilders, binders, paper-makers, and calligraphers labored shoulder to shoulder under the direct supervision of the shah or his princely relatives. What emerged were objects of staggering sophistication: the illustrated *Shahnameh* of Shah Tahmasp, the velvet carpets of Kashan and Tabriz, the tiled courtyards of Isfahan, the miniatures of Reza Abbasi. This chapter traces how a dynasty founded by sword-wielding Qizilbash warriors became, within a generation or two, the most sophisticated patron of the visual arts between Venice and Beijing. It is a story of synthesis - of how two great schools, Turkoman and Timurid, fused into something entirely new, and how that new thing came to define what the word "Persian" means in the imagination of the world.

The Tabriz School and the Shahnameh of Shah Tahmasp

When Shah Ismail rode into Tabriz in 1501 and proclaimed the Safavid dynasty, he inherited a city that had already been a capital of painting for more than a century. The Turkoman rulers who preceded him - the Aq Qoyunlu - had cultivated a school of manuscript illustration marked by bold color, dramatic landscapes, and crowded compositions bursting with energy. But Ismail was not content with what Tabriz already had.

In 1510 he defeated the Uzbeks at Merv and took Herat, the glittering Timurid capital in Khorasan. Herat had been the center of a very different artistic tradition: refined, elegant, almost introspective, obsessed with psychological nuance and compositional restraint. Its master was Kamal al-Din Behzad, already a legend in his own lifetime. Ismail did what conquerors of that era routinely did with skilled artisans. He packed them up and marched them west.

The migration of Herati painters to Tabriz produced one of the most consequential collisions in the history of art. Turkoman flamboyance met Timurid delicacy, and out of the friction came what historians now call the Safavid style - a fusion that would dominate Persian painting for two centuries. Colors deepened. Figures grew more individualized. Landscapes became extravagant gardens in which every blade of grass seemed individually considered, yet the whole still pulsed with Turkoman drama.

The supreme monument of this synthesis is the *Shahnameh* of Shah Tahmasp, sometimes called the Houghton Shahnameh after a twentieth-century owner. Commissioned by Ismail for his young son and carried to completion under Tahmasp himself, it took roughly two decades to produce, from the 1520s into the 1540s. It contains 258 miniatures, each one a separate small masterpiece. Dozens of the finest painters in Iran contributed to it, working under the direction of figures like Sultan Muhammad, whose painting *The Court of Gayumars* - the mythical first king of Iran surrounded by a court clothed in leopard skins amid mountains dissolving into swirling clouds - is often cited as the single greatest Persian miniature ever produced.

The book was a political document as much as an artistic one. The *Shahnameh*, Ferdowsi's thousand-year-old epic of Iranian kings, legitimized the Safavids by placing them in a line stretching back to mythical antiquity. To illustrate it lavishly was to claim that heritage visually, to announce that the new Shi'i dynasty was the rightful heir of every Iranian monarch who had ever worn a crown. Tahmasp oversaw the project personally, occasionally taking up brushes himself - he had trained as a painter in his youth, an unusual education for a shah and one that left him permanently attuned to the craft.

Then, somewhere in his middle years, Tahmasp lost interest. Historians have puzzled over this for centuries. He grew more religious, more austere, more suspicious of worldly pleasures. He issued edicts of repentance. He dismissed artists from the royal workshop or sent them on reduced allowances. The great *Shahnameh* itself he eventually gave away, dispatched as a diplomatic gift to the Ottoman sultan Selim II in 1568 along with a Quran and other treasures. It was perhaps the most extraordinary act of artistic regifting in human history. The book vanished into the Ottoman treasury and from there, centuries later, into the private market, where its pages were broken apart and scattered across the world's museums - a dispersal that mirrored, in a way, the wider dispersal of Safavid style itself.

Behzad's Legacy and the Royal Kitabkhana

Behzad arrived in Tabriz as a living monument. Already elderly when Ismail brought him from Herat, he had painted for the Timurid sultan Husayn Bayqara and had watched the last great flowering of that eastern court. By the 1520s, Shah Ismail had appointed him director of the royal *kitabkhana*, and Behzad became, in effect, the curator of Iranian visual memory.

His influence operated less through individual paintings than through the generations he trained. The Safavid *kitabkhana* was an extraordinary institution: part workshop, part academy, part bureaucratic department. Paper came from Samarkand or was manufactured locally in specialist mills. Pigments were ground from lapis lazuli hauled across mountains from Badakhshan, from malachite, cinnabar, orpiment, and powdered gold. Each color had its specialist. Outlines were drawn by master designers, backgrounds filled by apprentices, faces and hands finished by the most senior hands. A single folio might pass through a dozen pairs of hands over months.

That system meant style was inherited like a family trade. A painter trained in the *kitabkhana* absorbed not just techniques but habits of seeing - how to compose a battle, how to tilt a head to suggest listening, how to build a hillside out of interlocking strokes that read as both rock and abstraction. Behzad's particular gifts - his attention to psychological expression, his crowded yet legible compositions, his deep interest in ordinary laborers and street life - seeped into the DNA of Safavid painting and stayed there.

After Behzad's death around 1535, leadership of the workshops passed to figures like Mir Musavvir and his son Mir Sayyid Ali. When Tahmasp's enthusiasm waned, some of these artists left for more welcoming courts. The Mughal emperor Humayun, during his exile in Iran, recruited Mir Sayyid Ali and another Safavid master, Abd al-Samad, to help found what would become the Mughal painting tradition in India. The Safavid *kitabkhana* thus seeded empires far beyond its own borders.

Inside Iran, patronage devolved to princes. Tahmasp's nephew Ibrahim Mirza, governor of Mashhad, inherited both the shah's collection of artists and his taste for beautiful books. Between 1556 and 1565, Ibrahim Mirza's workshop produced the *Haft Awrang*, or Seven Thrones, of the poet Jami - a manuscript many scholars consider the equal of Tahmasp's *Shahnameh* in sheer quality of illustration. Ibrahim Mirza himself was murdered in a palace purge in 1577, his library dispersed, his painters scattered. The story of Safavid art, like the story of the dynasty itself, was one of brilliance repeatedly interrupted by politics and repeatedly reconstituted somewhere else.

Reza Abbasi and the Single-Page Painting

When Shah Abbas I moved his capital to Isfahan in 1598, Safavid art underwent a second revolution. The age of the great illustrated manuscript was ending. Books took decades and fortunes to produce, and the new age had less patience and different appetites. In its place arose a new form: the single-sheet painting, meant to be collected into albums called *muraqqa*, passed between connoisseurs, admired in private gatherings, discussed like poems.

The artist who defined this form was Reza Abbasi. Born around 1565 to a painter father, he emerged in the last decades of the sixteenth century as the most distinctive Persian hand of his generation. Shah Abbas recognized his talent and granted him the honorific "Abbasi" - the shah's own name attached to the painter's, a rare and intimate honor. For a while Reza worked in the royal workshop. Then, in a move that scandalized the court chroniclers, he walked away.

The contemporary historian Qazi Ahmad wrote that Reza began frequenting wrestlers and lowlifes, dressing like a vagrant, spending his time in the coffeehouses and athletic clubs of Isfahan rather than the palace. Whether this was spiritual rebellion, personal crisis, or simply a change in economic circumstances - since the single-sheet market now offered a living outside royal patronage - his work from this period shows an artist enormously confident in his own vision.

Reza's paintings are like nothing that came before. Where earlier Persian miniatures were crowded panoramas, his are studies in isolation: a single elegant youth leaning against a tree, a dervish squatting on bare ground, a calligrapher at work, a pair of lovers entwined. The line is everything. His drawings breathe. A single continuous stroke might define an entire turban, curl through a shoulder, and end in the curve of a sleeve. Backgrounds are minimal or absent. Color is used sparingly, sometimes only as a wash of gold or a touch of blue.

His subjects were often what an earlier age would have considered unworthy: handsome boys, courtesans, European travelers, ordinary craftsmen. Portugal and Holland had arrived in the Persian Gulf, and European visitors in wide hats and peculiar coats began appearing in Reza's album leaves, depicted with curious anthropological precision. This was Iran looking at the world and at itself with a new kind of relaxed, almost ironic self-awareness.

Reza returned to royal favor in his later years and died in 1635, having trained a generation of followers - including his own son Muhammad Shafi Abbasi - who carried his style into the seventeenth century. His paintings commanded extraordinary prices in his own lifetime. A single page might cost more than a horse. Collectors competed for his work the way later Europeans would compete for Rembrandt drawings, and for similar reasons: each sheet was understood to be the direct trace of a unique hand.

The cultural implications were profound. Reza Abbasi turned the Persian painter from a skilled workshop hand into something closer to what we would now call an artist - an individual whose signature carried value, whose personality infused the work, whose biography mattered. The modern idea of an art market, of authorship, of collectible originals, found an early and remarkably full expression in the salons of Safavid Isfahan.

Calligraphy as the Highest Art

To understand why calligraphers were honored above generals, one must understand what writing meant in a culture whose sacred text was the Arabic Quran and whose literary glory was Persian poetry. The letter itself was holy. To form it beautifully was an act of devotion, and to do so at the highest level was a form of grace granted by God to a very few.

The Safavid era produced calligraphers whose names were spoken in the same breath as the great poets. Sultan Ali Mashhadi, whose career spanned the late Timurid and early Safavid periods, perfected the flowing script called *nastaliq* - the "bride of Islamic calligraphies," a style so graceful it seemed to lean forward as it moved across the page. His work became the standard against which all later *nastaliq* was measured.

A century later, under Shah Abbas, Mir Emad al-Hasani raised the art to what many still consider its absolute peak. His letters have a crystalline precision - each curve mathematically exact, each proportion perfectly weighed - combined with an energy that makes the page seem almost alive. Shah Abbas valued him enormously but also, according to the sources, came to resent his independent personality and his reputed Sunni sympathies. In 1615, Mir Emad was murdered in Isfahan, reportedly with the shah's tacit approval. His assassination became a byword for the dangerous proximity of genius to power.

The economics tell the story as clearly as the aesthetics. A single couplet copied in Mir Emad's hand could sell for a gold coin. A full manuscript was a fortune. Courtiers and merchants built entire album collections around calligraphic specimens, mounting them on decorated borders, arranging them in dialogue with paintings. The *muraqqa* album was, in a sense, the Safavid invention of the curated exhibition.

Calligraphy also structured the other arts. Painters studied calligraphic line as the foundation of drawing. Architects incorporated monumental inscriptions - Quranic verses, royal titulatures, poetic fragments - into tile friezes that wrapped whole buildings in ribbons of text. Potters signed their finest work in looping *nastaliq*. The pen was not one art among many. It was the root from which the others grew, and its masters were accorded a reverence that modern secular cultures reserve for no one at all.

Carpets, Tilework, and Textile Mastery

While the painters worked in the palace, other Safavid artists worked on a scale that could cover an entire floor or clothe an entire mosque. The age produced the greatest carpets ever woven, tilework of almost incomprehensible complexity, and silks and velvets that still rank among the most technically accomplished textiles in human history.

The Ardabil Carpet, woven in 1539-1540 during Tahmasp's reign, is the most famous. Two were originally made as a matching pair for the shrine of Shaykh Safi al-Din, the founding saint of the Safavid order, at Ardabil. One is now in the Victoria and Albert Museum in London; its damaged twin, partly cannibalized to repair the first, is in Los Angeles. The London carpet measures nearly thirty-five feet by eighteen. Its center is a single vast medallion - the hanging lamp of a mosque reflected as if in still water - surrounded by an infinity of scrolling vines. It contains roughly twenty-six million knots. A Persian couplet woven into one end names the designer, Maqsud of Kashan, and dates the work.

The Ardabil was not a folk object. It was designed by court artists, drawn onto cartoons the size of the finished piece, and woven by teams of specialist weavers. Its patterns echo the illumination of contemporary Qurans. Here lies one of the deepest truths about Safavid art: the same designers worked across media. A motif developed in a manuscript border might reappear on a carpet, then on a tile panel, then on a silk robe. The culture had a single visual vocabulary expressed in a hundred materials.

Carpet weaving flourished in Kashan, Kerman, Isfahan, and Tabriz. Under Shah Abbas, royal workshops produced carpets specifically for export, and Armenian merchants based in New Julfa carried them to Venice, Lisbon, and Amsterdam, where they hung on the walls of

European palaces and appeared in the paintings of Vermeer and Holbein. A Persian carpet became, in Europe, the universal symbol of oriental luxury - a reputation it has never entirely lost.

Tilework performed a similar function on a larger scale. The mosques and palaces of Isfahan, particularly the Masjid-i Shah and the Shaykh Lutfullah Mosque, wrapped vast architectural surfaces in tiled mosaic. The cuerda seca technique, in which colored glazes were separated by a greasy line that burned away in firing, allowed faster production than traditional mosaic at a slight cost in sharpness. The domes of Isfahan, glowing turquoise and indigo and ochre in the desert sun, were walls of painting expanded to architectural scale.

Silks and velvets were the third great Safavid textile achievement. Kashan and Yazd produced figural silks of astonishing complexity, depicting scenes of lovers in gardens, hunters pursuing deer, or European travelers in their odd clothes - the same repertoire, in other words, that Reza Abbasi was drawing on paper. Some surviving pieces use seven or more colors of silk thread with gold and silver wire, woven in patterns so fine the weavers must have worked at the very edge of what human eyesight could achieve. A single cloak for Shah Abbas could take a year to weave. He wore such cloaks to diplomatic audiences, where they served exactly the function the Safavids wanted them to serve: to announce, without words, that Iran stood at the summit of civilization.

Analysis

What the Safavids understood, perhaps better than any contemporary dynasty, was that beauty is a form of power. Their empire faced rivals on every border - Ottomans to the west, Uzbeks to the east, eventually Mughals to the southeast - and could not always win on the battlefield. But it could win on the page, the loom, and the tiled wall. A *Shahnameh* given to an Ottoman sultan was a kind of disarmament, an acknowledgment that certain contests were over before they began, because no Ottoman workshop could produce its equal.

Artistic integration also mirrored, and helped to create, the integration of Iran itself. Turkoman energy and Timurid refinement fused into a single visual language that transcended the regional origins of either. When Europeans in the seventeenth century began to speak of a distinct "Persian style" in painting, carpets, and architecture, they were recognizing something the Safavids had deliberately built. A cultural identity had been manufactured in the workshops of Tabriz and Isfahan as surely as a political one had been forged on the battlefields of Chaldiran and Herat.

And the art outlived the empire. When the Safavid state collapsed in 1722, the paintings, carpets, and tiles remained, and the visual vocabulary they established became the inheritance of every subsequent Iranian dynasty and of Persian-speaking cultures from Delhi to Istanbul. In a very real sense, modern Iran still sees itself through Safavid eyes.

Key Figures & Events

- **Kamal al-Din Behzad** - Herat master brought to Tabriz, director of the royal *kitabkhana*, whose influence shaped generations.

- **Sultan Muhammad** - leading painter of Tahmasp's *Shahnameh*, creator of *The Court of Gayumars*.

- **Shah Tahmasp** - trained painter, royal patron, and eventual giver-away of his own masterpieces.

- **Ibrahim Mirza** - Tahmasp's nephew and patron of the *Haft Awrang*, murdered in 1577.

- **Reza Abbasi** - pioneer of the single-sheet painting and the modern Persian artistic persona.

- **Mir Emad al-Hasani** - supreme master of *nastaliq* calligraphy, murdered in 1615.

- **The Ardabil Carpet (1539-40)** - the most celebrated surviving Safavid carpet, woven for the dynastic shrine.

Quick Summary

- Shah Ismail's conquest of Herat in 1510 brought Timurid masters like Behzad to Tabriz, fusing eastern and western schools into a new Safavid style.

- The *Shahnameh* of Shah Tahmasp, with 258 miniatures produced over two decades, is the supreme monument of Safavid manuscript art.

- The royal *kitabkhana* functioned as a workshop-academy whose trained masters seeded the Mughal painting tradition in India.

- Under Shah Abbas I, Reza Abbasi invented a new art of single-sheet paintings prized for their individual authorship and collected in albums.

- Calligraphers like Sultan Ali Mashhadi and Mir Emad al-Hasani were honored above generals; the pen was considered the root art of the civilization.

- The Ardabil Carpet of 1539-40 exemplifies a golden age of Persian weaving that supplied both royal shrines and European markets.

- Tilework at Isfahan's great mosques and silk textiles from Kashan and Yazd extended the same visual vocabulary across every scale of life.

- Safavid art was deliberate soft power: a way to claim Iranian cultural supremacy over Ottoman, Uzbek, and Mughal rivals.

Long after the last Safavid shah had been driven from his throne, the objects his ancestors commissioned continued to do their work. They hung in the palaces of enemies, were copied in the workshops of successors, and gradually, over centuries, came to define in the global imagination what Iran was and is. An empire that was often defeated in war won, unambiguously, in beauty - and in that victory built one of the most durable cultural identities the world has known.

An empire often defeated in war won unambiguously in beauty, and in that victory built a cultural identity that would outlast every throne. But the Safavid workshops were not only producing tilework and miniatures. In the same decades that Reza Abbasi was painting courtiers into immortality, scholars in the seminaries of Isfahan were assembling a philosophical and legal synthesis every bit as durable as the domes. The pen competed with the brush for Safavid attention, and what it produced would shape how Iranians thought about God, reason, and authority long after the last royal manuscript had been sealed into a library.

Chapter 12:

Mullahs, Mystics, and the Shi'i Synthesis

In the same decades that René Descartes was sitting beside a Dutch stove writing *Cogito, ergo sum*, a bearded scholar in the Iranian highlands was composing a four-volume treatise on the metaphysics of being that would shape Muslim thought for the next four centuries. His name was Sadr al-Din Shirazi, known to history as Mulla Sadra. Almost no European has heard of him. Almost every Iranian philosopher since has had to reckon with him.

The Safavid century was not only an age of cannon and silk. It was also one of the most fertile periods of religious and philosophical creativity in Islamic history, a moment when a freshly imposed state religion - Twelver Shi'ism - had to be built from the ground up. There were not enough Shi'i clerics in Iran in 1501 to staff a single madrasa properly. By 1700 there was a vast clerical establishment, a sophisticated jurisprudence, a mystical philosophy of breathtaking ambition, and a popular devotional culture that still defines Iranian religion today. What follows traces how a heterodox dervish movement that conquered Iran on horseback ended up producing both Mulla Sadra's metaphysics and Muhammad Baqir Majlisi's law books - and how those two strands, the mystical and the legal, fought for the soul of Iranian Shi'ism.

Building a Shi'i Clerical Establishment

When Shah Ismail rode into Tabriz in 1501 and announced that Twelver Shi'ism would henceforth be the religion of his realm, he confronted an awkward problem. The Iranian plateau was overwhelmingly Sunni. The few Shi'i communities that existed were scattered, and the existing clerical infrastructure - the madrasas, the prayer leaders, the judges - was Sunni to its bones. Worse still, the new shah's own court religion was a wild, messianic blend of Sufi devotion to the Safavid family and apocalyptic expectation. It bore only a passing resemblance to the careful jurisprudence of the Twelver scholars of southern Iraq and Lebanon.

To build a state religion you need clerics who can articulate it. Ismail and his successors imported them. Shi'i scholars from the Arab heartlands of Twelver learning - especially Jabal Amil in present-day Lebanon, and the shrine cities of Najaf and Karbala - were enticed to Iran with stipends, land grants, and prestige. The most famous of these immigrants, Ali al-Karaki, became something close to a state theologian under Shah Tahmasp, with the formal title of Deputy of the Hidden Imam. That phrase carried a thunderclap of meaning. The Twelfth Imam, occulted since 874, was the only legitimate ruler of the Muslim community. To call a living scholar his deputy was to claim that learned jurists could exercise his authority on earth - and, by extension, that the shah ruled with their blessing rather than in his own right.

This was a quiet revolution. In earlier Twelver thought the imam's absence had been a kind of paralysis: nothing public could be done in his name. The Safavid clerical establishment slowly chipped away at that paralysis. Friday prayer, long suspended in the imam's absence, was reinstated under clerical leadership. Religious taxes - the *khums*, one fifth of certain forms of income - began to flow into the hands of senior scholars rather than waiting indefinitely for a returning messiah. Sharia courts proliferated. A bureaucracy of state-appointed religious officials, headed by the *sadr*, distributed endowments and supervised orthodoxy.

By the reign of Shah Abbas I (1588-1629), the rough outlines of an entirely new institution were visible: a salaried, propertied, scholarly elite with its own networks, its own seminaries, and its own claim to interpret divine law. The shah encouraged this elite because it gave his hybrid empire a unifying religious identity and a buffer against the Ottomans, who claimed the leadership of Sunni Islam. But he also kept it on a short leash, controlling appointments and patronage. The clerics knew their power was real. They also knew it depended, for now, on the crown.

Two unresolved tensions hummed beneath this construction project. First, what was the proper relationship between rational philosophy - the inheritance of Avicenna and the Greeks - and the revealed traditions of the imams? Second, what was to be done with the Sufi orders, including the Safavid order itself, whose ecstatic devotions had brought the dynasty to power but sat uneasily with sober jurisprudence? Different scholars answered differently, and their answers shaped the next two centuries.

Mulla Sadra and the School of Isfahan

Sadr al-Din Muhammad Shirazi was born around 1571 into a wealthy Shirazi family. His father was a high official with no other male heir; the boy was raised with every advantage. He moved to Qazvin around 1591 to study under the leading scholars of the Safavid capital, then followed them to Isfahan in 1597 when Shah Abbas transferred his court there. Isfahan was at that moment becoming one of the most exciting intellectual cities in the world. Mulla Sadra threw himself into its three competing currents: Peripatetic philosophy in the Avicennan tradition, the illuminationist mysticism of Suhrawardi, and the visionary Sufism of Ibn al-Arabi. His genius was to braid them together.

His teacher Mir Damad - the so-called Third Teacher, after Aristotle and al-Farabi - had begun the synthesis. Mulla Sadra carried it into territory no Muslim philosopher had quite reached. The result is the system he called *al-hikma al-muta'aliya*, the Transcendent Wisdom, set out in his vast magnum opus *The Four Journeys*, written between 1606 and 1628 and revised until his death in 1635.

141

His central claim is deceptively simple. Existence, he argued, is the fundamental reality. Essence - the whatness of a thing, its definition - is a mental abstraction. Real things are not first defined and then granted being; they exist first, and our minds grasp their essences afterward. From this starting point Mulla Sadra built an entire metaphysics of motion. Existence, he insisted, is graded - more intense in some beings, less in others, like light shining at varying brightnesses from a single source. And existence is dynamic. Things do not merely change their properties; they undergo what he called substantial motion, an unbroken intensification of being itself, in which the soul ascends through degrees of reality toward its source.

None of this was abstract gymnastics. Mulla Sadra was trying to reconcile, on a single ladder of being, the rationalism of the philosophers, the visionary disclosures of the mystics, and the revelations of the Quran and the imams. The ascent of the philosopher's mind, the ascent of the Sufi's heart, and the ascent of the prophet's spirit were all, for him, motions along the same vertical axis. He was, in a sense, doing in Persian what no European thinker would attempt: holding together reason and ecstasy in one rigorously argued system.

This did not please everyone. The literalist clerics of Shiraz drove him out of the city for what they considered dangerous innovations. He spent years in retreat in the village of Kahak near Qom, fasting and meditating, before being recalled by a more sympathetic patron to teach in Shiraz. He died, according to tradition, in Basra in 1635 while returning from his seventh pilgrimage to Mecca on foot.

The school he founded - usually called the School of Isfahan, though its members studied across Iran - did not vanish with him. His students Mulla Muhsin Fayz Kashani and Abd al-Razzaq Lahiji extended his work into theology and ethics. His texts became the backbone of advanced philosophical training in Iranian seminaries, where they remain today. When the Ayatollah Khomeini lectured on philosophy in Qom in the 1930s, the text on his lectern was Mulla Sadra. When contemporary Iranian intellectuals argue about modernity and tradition, they argue, often without knowing it, in Sadrian categories. Few thinkers have shaped a national mind so thoroughly while remaining so completely unknown abroad.

Majlisi and the Triumph of Legalism

Muhammad Baqir Majlisi was born in Isfahan in 1627, the son of a respected scholar, and he would die there in 1699 as the most powerful cleric the Safavid Empire had yet produced. Where Mulla Sadra was a metaphysician of being, Majlisi was an encyclopedist of tradition. Where Sadra sought to ascend through degrees of reality toward the divine, Majlisi sought to gather, classify, and legislate every recorded saying of the Prophet and the imams.

His monument is the *Bihar al-Anwar*, the Oceans of Lights, a colossal compendium of Shi'i Hadith that runs to more than a hundred volumes in modern editions. It was nothing less than an attempt to gather the entire textual heritage of Twelver Shi'ism and arrange it under coherent headings: theology, prayer, ethics, history of the imams, eschatology, even cosmology. Majlisi composed shorter works in Persian for the literate laity, on subjects from ritual purity to the proper way to mourn the martyrs of Karbala. Through these vernacular books, much of the popular Shi'i devotional culture that survives in Iran today - the elaborate mourning processions of Muharram, the visits to imamzadeh shrines, the rituals of intercession - took its modern shape.

Majlisi rose under Shah Sulayman and reached the apex of his influence under the last effective Safavid, Shah Sultan Husayn, who appointed him *shaykh al-Islam* of Isfahan in 1687. From that office he wielded an authority no earlier Safavid cleric had matched. He pressed the shah to enforce Sharia with new rigor. He campaigned against wine drinking at court, against the religious minorities tolerated under Shah Abbas - Jews, Christians, Zoroastrians, who now faced new restrictions and pressures to convert - and, above all, against what he regarded as twin enemies of true Shi'ism: speculative philosophy and Sufism.

For Majlisi, Mulla Sadra's project was a dangerous distraction at best, an importation of Greek paganism at worst. The proper sources of religious knowledge were the Quran and the traditions of the imams, transmitted through chains of reliable narrators and interpreted by trained jurists. Reason had a role, but a subordinate one - a tool for parsing texts, not a ladder to God. The mystics' claim to direct experience of the divine he regarded as either self-delusion or fraud, and politically dangerous either way.

His success was striking. By the end of the seventeenth century the philosophical chairs of Isfahan were quieter. Manuscripts of Mulla Sadra were still copied, but they circulated within smaller, more cautious circles. The dominant tone of Safavid religion had become juristic, scriptural, and concerned above all with correct practice. Friday sermons, devotional poetry, the liturgies of Muharram - all bore the Majlisi stamp.

Historians have argued ever since about whether Majlisi's triumph was a stiffening of Iranian religion into rigidity or a necessary consolidation of a still-young state religion. He certainly gave Iranian Shi'ism a coherence and a popular reach it had previously lacked. He also narrowed it. The conversation Mulla Sadra had tried to keep open between reason, tradition, and mystical experience would have to be reopened, painfully, by later generations.

Suppressing the Sufis Who Founded the Dynasty

There is a peculiar irony at the heart of late Safavid religion. The dynasty had begun as a Sufi order. The Safaviyya of Ardabil, founded in the thirteenth century by Shaykh Safi al-Din, had grown over two centuries into a militant brotherhood whose murids - disciples - regarded its master as a living link to God. The Qizilbash warriors who placed Shah Ismail on the throne in 1501 had charged into battle shouting his name as a divine epithet. The Safavid claim to rule rested, originally, on this Sufi pedigree.

Yet by Majlisi's time the Sufis had become objects of clerical contempt and, increasingly, of state persecution. How did this happen?

The answer lies partly in the dynasty's own evolution. Shah Tahmasp had already begun to distance himself from the wilder Qizilbash devotionalism, leaning instead on the imported Arab jurists. Shah Abbas, building a centralized empire of slave soldiers and salaried officials, had even less use for tribal mystics whose loyalty was personal rather than institutional. As the shahs grew more orthodox in their public religion, the Sufi orders that had once been allies became politically suspect rivals. They had charisma the state could not control, networks that crossed provincial boundaries, and a habit of producing claimants to spiritual - and sometimes worldly - authority.

The clerics had their own reasons for hostility. Sufism, with its emphasis on direct experience of the divine and its literature of ecstatic love, had always sat uneasily with a jurisprudence built on transmitted texts. In the orthodox Twelver framework Majlisi was constructing, the only legitimate path to God ran through the imams and their scholarly heirs. The Sufi shaykhs were competitors for that mediating role. They were also, conveniently, vulnerable - many of their classical texts had been written by Sunnis, and many of their practices could be branded innovations.

The result was a sustained campaign. Khanaqahs, the lodges where Sufis gathered for meditation and music, were closed or repurposed in major cities. Polemical treatises poured from the pens of Majlisi and his allies, denouncing Sufism root and branch. Some orders were driven underground; others fled to India, where the Mughal court still welcomed mystics. The Nimatullahi order, one of the great Persian Sufi traditions, survived only by relocating to the Deccan for more than a century before tentatively returning in the late eighteenth century.

The Safavid family kept the title of head of the Safavi order, but the order itself withered. By 1700 the dynasty's mystical origins had been so thoroughly sanitized that they were almost an embarrassment. A

movement that had ridden Sufi devotion to power had ended by
outlawing the devotion that brought it there - one of the more striking
acts of self-erasure in the history of any ruling house.

The Foundations of Modern Shi'ism

By the time Afghan invaders sacked Isfahan in 1722 and brought the
Safavid dynasty crashing down, the religious world the dynasty had
built was largely set. Iran was Twelver Shi'i, and would remain so. The
clerical establishment had its salaries, its endowments, its seminaries
in Isfahan and Qom and the shrine cities of Iraq, and its accumulated
claim to act as deputies of the Hidden Imam. Popular religion centered
on the imams, on Karbala, on the shrines and the Muharram
processions Majlisi had codified. Philosophy survived in the
seminaries as a respected if often suspect specialty, transmitted through
Mulla Sadra's texts.

The political collapse of the Safavids did not undo any of this. If
anything, it strengthened the clerics. With no shah to lean on - and, for
long stretches in the eighteenth century, no effective state at all -
religious scholars became the most stable institution in Iranian life.
They controlled education, family law, and much of the charitable
economy. Senior figures residing in Najaf and Karbala, beyond the
reach of any Iranian government, could speak with an independence
that earlier shaykhs had never enjoyed.

The two strands the Safavid centuries had woven - the legalism of
Majlisi and the mysticism of Mulla Sadra - continued in uneasy
coexistence. Periodically one would surge and the other would recede,
only to return. In the nineteenth century a movement called the Usulis
decisively established the right of qualified jurists to exercise
independent reasoning, paving the way for the marja' al-taqlid - the
source of emulation - whose followers number in the millions today. In
the twentieth century Mulla Sadra's metaphysics was rediscovered by
intellectuals seeking an indigenous response to Western modernity, and

his ideas saturated the philosophical formation of the men who would lead the 1979 revolution.

Key Figures & Events

Ali al-Karaki imported Twelver jurisprudence from Jabal Amil and gave the early Safavid state its legal scaffolding. Mir Damad founded the philosophical revival of Isfahan under Shah Abbas. Mulla Sadra (c. 1571-1635) created the most ambitious metaphysical synthesis in Islamic history. Muhammad Baqir Majlisi (1627-1699) compiled the *Bihar al-Anwar* and crushed Sufism and speculative philosophy from his post as *shaykh al-Islam* of Isfahan. Across the same two centuries, a Shi'i clerical establishment grew from almost nothing into a wealthy, self-governing institution able to outlast the dynasty that created it.

Analysis

The Safavid religious project succeeded almost too well. The empire forged a Shi'i Iran so durable that nearly every later Iranian regime, secular or religious, has had to reckon with it. But the success had a price. The cosmopolitan philosophical conversation Mulla Sadra had tried to sustain - between Greek reason, Sufi vision, and revealed law - was narrowed by Majlisi's triumph into something closer to a clerical monopoly on truth. The mystical orders that had given the dynasty its energy were driven into the shadows. The result was a religion of remarkable coherence and remarkable rigidity, capable of mobilizing entire populations around the memory of Karbala but suspicious of intellectual freedoms it had once nurtured. The tension between Sadra and Majlisi - between the metaphysician and the canonist - was never resolved. It was inherited.

Quick Summary

- The Safavids built a Twelver Shi'i clerical establishment from scratch, importing Arab jurists and granting them unprecedented authority as deputies of the Hidden Imam.

- Under Shah Abbas, Isfahan became a major center of philosophical and mystical thought, home to thinkers like Mir Damad and Mulla Sadra.

- Mulla Sadra (c. 1571-1635) created the Transcendent Wisdom, fusing Avicennan philosophy, Suhrawardi's illuminationism, and Ibn al-Arabi's mysticism into a system still central to Iranian thought.

- Muhammad Baqir Majlisi (1627-1699) compiled the vast *Bihar al-Anwar* Hadith collection and championed a juristic, scriptural Shi'ism over speculative philosophy.

- Majlisi's policies shaped popular Iranian religion - especially the rituals of Muharram and shrine devotion - that continue today.

- The Safavid state turned against Sufism, including the dynasty's own founding order, closing lodges and persecuting mystical brotherhoods.

- The clerical establishment built under the Safavids outlived the dynasty and became the most durable institution in Iranian society.

- The unresolved tension between Mulla Sadra's mysticism and Majlisi's legalism still structures Iranian religious life in the twenty-first century.

Walk into a seminary in Qom today and you will find young clerics arguing, as their predecessors did three hundred years ago, over the relative authority of reason, tradition, and mystical insight. The vocabulary is Sadra's; the institutional framework is Majlisi's; the underlying tension was forged in the workshops of Safavid Isfahan. Empires fall, but the categories they bequeath to their heirs can outlast any throne. The Crimson Crown lost its head in 1722. The religious world it had built was only beginning.

Empires fall, but the categories they bequeath to their heirs can outlast any throne. The philosophical vocabulary of Mulla Sadra and the legal framework of Majlisi were the high achievements of Safavid thought, but they were not the whole of what the dynasty left behind. Beneath the debates of the seminaries, beneath the decrees of the shahs and the ledgers of the Armenian merchants, ran a slower current: the rhythms of ordinary life in streets and kitchens and teahouses, in Nowruz celebrations and Muharram processions. An Englishman who watched a procession in Isfahan in 1617 glimpsed what the court chronicles rarely recorded.

Chapter 13:

Life in the Empire

In the spring of 1617, an English traveler named Thomas Herbert watched a procession in Isfahan and confessed he had never seen a city so alive. Drums, horsemen, women peering from lattice windows, the scent of saffron rice drifting from a thousand kitchens. Empires, he realized, are not built in throne rooms. They are built in streets.

The Safavid state followed so far has been a story of shahs and shaykhs, of qizilbash cavalry and Qandahar's walls. But for every soldier in Shah Abbas's army there were a hundred weavers, farmers, camel drovers, and mothers whose names never reached a chronicle. Their Iran was a mosaic of Persians and Armenians, Georgians and Kurds, Arabs of the Gulf and Turkmens of the steppe, Jews in their mahalleh and Zoroastrians tending fires in remote Yazd. Understanding how these people ate, worshipped, married, mourned, and celebrated is the only way to grasp what the Safavids actually made. A dynasty can decree a state religion; it cannot decree what happens on a Tuesday afternoon at the bazaar. The empire's real achievement was not conquest but the slow knitting together of these daily worlds into something recognizably, enduringly Iranian.

Cities, Villages, and Nomads

Safavid Iran was a land of three societies stacked uneasily on one another. The city, the village, and the tent each had its own calendar, its own loyalties, and its own relationship to the shah in Isfahan.

The great cities - Tabriz, Qazvin, Isfahan, Shiraz, Mashhad - were extraordinary by the standards of the age. Isfahan under Shah Abbas I swelled to perhaps half a million people, rivaling London and Paris combined. At its heart sprawled the Maidan-i Naqsh-i Jahan, a vast rectangle the size of several football fields, bordered by the Shah Mosque, the Lutfallah Mosque, the Ali Qapu palace, and the grand bazaar. A visitor could buy Chinese porcelain and Venetian glass within minutes of each other, haggle in Turkish, conclude in Persian, and settle the bill in silver abbasi coins that circulated from Aleppo to Surat.

The bazaar was not simply a market. It was a guild system, a court of commercial law, a charitable institution, and a neighborhood. Each trade occupied its own covered lane - coppersmiths here, silk merchants there, bookbinders and papermakers in another quarter. The *kadkhoda*, or guild elder, mediated disputes and collected taxes. Above him stood the *muhtasib*, the market inspector, who checked weights and prices and could flog a baker caught adulterating his flour.

Most Iranians, however, never saw Isfahan. They lived in villages of mud-brick houses clustered around a mosque, a bathhouse, and the vital *qanat* - the underground irrigation channel that had watered the Iranian plateau since antiquity. Peasants owed a share of their crop, often a third or more, to a landlord who might be a local notable, a religious endowment, or the crown itself. Wheat and barley were the staples; in better land, rice, cotton, and the precious silk cocoons that Shah Abbas would turn into the empire's most valuable export.

Village life was hard and close to the bone. A bad harvest meant hunger; a good one meant a wedding and perhaps a new copper pot. But villages were not isolated. Itinerant dervishes passed through with news and blessings. Tax collectors arrived with depressing regularity. And on certain days each year, the village road filled with a third kind of Iranian: the nomad.

Tribal confederations - Shahsevan, Bakhtiari, Qashqai, Kurdish clans, Lur pastoralists - moved their flocks between summer pastures in the mountains and winter grazing in the lowlands. They paid tribute in sheep and, when the shah required, in soldiers. The qizilbash themselves had begun as such tribesmen, and the tension between settled administrators in Isfahan and the tented aristocracy of the hills never fully resolved. A Kurdish chief in his felt tent considered himself as Iranian as any bazaar merchant - and perhaps, he would have said, rather more free.

These three worlds traded constantly. City bread depended on village wheat; village flocks depended on nomad breeding; nomad tents were furnished with city cloth. The empire was the network that bound them.

Women, Family, and the Royal Harem

For a Safavid woman, life was largely lived behind a wall - but the wall was never quite as solid as foreign travelers, squinting from outside, liked to imagine.

Islamic law gave women defined rights: to inherit property, to own and manage their own wealth, to initiate divorce under specific conditions, to stipulate terms in their marriage contracts. Court records from Isfahan and Ardabil show women suing to recover dowries, disputing inheritances with brothers, and lending money at interest. A widow of means could be a formidable figure in her neighborhood, endowing a mosque or a bathhouse in her own name.

Marriage was arranged, usually within the extended family or the same trade or tribe. Girls married young, often at fourteen or fifteen; boys a few years later. The bride brought a dowry of textiles, copper, and jewelry, while the groom paid a *mahr*, a sum legally owed to the wife and often held in reserve against divorce. Polygamy was permitted but in practice uncommon outside the elite - most men could not afford a second household. Temporary marriage, *sigheh*, sanctioned by Twelver Shi'ism, offered a legal framework that ranged from genuine companionship to thinly veiled prostitution near shrines and caravanserais.

Inside the home, women ruled. They managed the kitchen and its stores, supervised children, negotiated with peddlers at the door, and hosted other women in elaborate afternoon gatherings. The public bathhouse, the *hammam*, was the great social institution of female life - a place for gossip, matchmaking, the inspection of prospective brides, and hours of ritual cleansing perfumed with rosewater. Men and women attended at different times, and a woman's hammam day was sacred.

Veiling practices varied by class, region, and period. Urban women wore the *chador* in the street; village women working in the fields wore far less. Under Shah Abbas, European travelers were often surprised by how visible Iranian women could be on certain occasions - at festivals, on pilgrimages, at royal ceremonies where queens and princesses sometimes appeared in curtained litters.

The royal harem was the most misunderstood institution of the empire. To European eyes it was a den of languid concubines; in reality it was a small city. Hundreds of women lived inside the palace complex in Isfahan - wives, concubines, mothers and aunts and sisters of the shah, their attendants, female officials, eunuchs, teachers, musicians. It had its own bureaucracy, treasury, and schools. Princes spent their early years there, tutored by mothers and eunuchs, and what they learned - or failed to learn - about the world beyond its walls would shape the empire for generations.

From the late sixteenth century, as Shah Abbas moved to keep potential rival princes under surveillance, young Safavid males were increasingly confined to the harem rather than sent out to govern provinces. The unintended consequence was profound. Mothers and senior women of the harem - the *valideh sultan* chief among them - became kingmakers, shaping succession, brokering marriages, and directing patronage. By the reign of Shah Sulayman in the later seventeenth century, court factions organized themselves around harem networks as surely as they did around viziers and generals.

Women also shaped piety. Wealthy women endowed mosques, madrasas, and bathhouses; ordinary women filled the shrines of Imam Reza at Mashhad and Fatima Ma'suma at Qom, weeping at the grilles of the tombs, tying strips of cloth to windows in petition. Historians have often written the Safavid story as a tale of men in turbans and armor. It was also, quietly and decisively, a tale of women in black and rose silk.

Religious Minorities: Christians, Jews, and Zoroastrians

Twelver Shi'ism was the state religion, enforced from above with a vigor that had no precedent in Iranian history. And yet the empire Shah Ismail built, and Shah Abbas consolidated, was a multi-religious one. A walk through Isfahan in 1620 would take you past a Shi'ite madrasa, an Armenian cathedral, a Jewish quarter, and within a day's ride, villages of Zoroastrians still tending the fires their ancestors had kindled before Islam arrived.

The Armenians were the most visible minority. Shah Abbas forcibly relocated tens of thousands of them from Julfa on the Aras River to a new suburb of Isfahan called New Julfa in 1604-1605. It was a brutal deportation - many died on the march - but the aim was economic. Abbas wanted Armenian merchants, with their networks stretching from Venice to Madras, to channel the world's silver into his silk trade. He gave them land, religious liberty, and a degree of self-government under their own *kalantar*, or mayor. They built churches - the Vank Cathedral still stands, its interior a dizzying fusion of Persian tilework and European biblical frescoes - and grew rich. New Julfan Armenians became, for a century, among the most successful commercial communities in Eurasia.

Jews had lived in Iran since the Babylonian exile, in communities from Hamadan to Shiraz to Kashan. Under Shi'ite law they were *dhimmi*, protected but subordinate, paying the *jizya* tax and subject to periodic indignities: distinctive clothing, restrictions on riding horses, prohibitions against entering bazaars on rainy days lest their supposed ritual impurity contaminate Muslims. Their fortunes rose and fell with particular shahs. Under Abbas I and his successor Safi, they were largely left alone; under Abbas II in the 1650s, they suffered a wave of forced conversions promoted by zealous clerics, and whole communities outwardly adopted Islam while maintaining Jewish practice in secret, the so-called *anusim*. When pressure eased, many returned openly to Judaism.

Despite these pressures, Jewish life persisted and at moments flourished. Judeo-Persian poetry reached extraordinary heights in this period; the poet Babai ben Lutf left a verse chronicle of his community's sufferings under Abbas II that remains one of the great documents of Iranian Jewish history.

Zoroastrians, the heirs of Iran's pre-Islamic faith, faced the hardest circumstances. Once the religion of empire, now a rural minority concentrated around Yazd and Kerman, they were often regarded by Shi'ite clerics as idolaters rather than a properly protected religious community. They paid heavy taxes, faced severe social restrictions, and saw periodic waves of forced conversion. Their sacred fires - some said to have burned for centuries without interruption - were hidden in modest compounds behind high walls. It was during the Safavid period that emigration to India accelerated, swelling the Parsi communities of Gujarat and Bombay that would become so prosperous in the British era.

Sunni Muslims, who had formed the majority of Iran's population in 1501, were a different problem. Aggressive Shi'ification - sometimes by preaching and patronage, sometimes by the sword - reshaped the religious map over two centuries. By 1700 most of the plateau was solidly Shi'ite, while Sunni communities survived mainly at the edges: among Kurds, Baluch, Turkmens, and in parts of the Gulf coast. The violence of this transformation, largely invisible in court chronicles, was one of the empire's most consequential legacies.

For all its pressures, Safavid Iran sustained a religious diversity that would have been unimaginable in contemporary Spain or England. Armenians worshipped openly in their cathedrals, Jews sang their liturgies, Zoroastrians kept their fires. Coexistence was unequal and often humiliating. It was also real.

Food, Coffee, and the Culture of Leisure

The Iranian table in 1650 would be instantly familiar to anyone who has eaten in Tehran or Tabriz today. Long-grained rice, pilau style, cooked with a golden crust at the bottom of the pot. Lamb stewed with dried limes, split peas, or pomegranate molasses and walnuts. Flatbreads - *sangak* baked on hot pebbles, *lavash* as thin as paper - torn by hand and used as spoon and plate. Yogurt thinned with water and mint. Sweet melons chilled in cold water from the qanat.

Food was hierarchy and hospitality both. A wealthy Isfahani household might serve a dozen dishes on a spread cloth; a peasant family in Fars made do with bread, cheese, herbs, and whatever the garden gave. But the code of hospitality was universal. A guest, even an enemy, was fed. Travelers' accounts marvel again and again at the generosity they met in villages too poor to feed themselves properly.

The great novelty of the seventeenth century was coffee. It arrived from the Arabian and Ottoman lands in the early 1600s and spread with astonishing speed. By the 1620s Isfahan had dozens of *qahveh-khaneh*, coffeehouses, and by mid-century they were one of the defining institutions of urban life. Men gathered on low platforms covered in carpets to drink small cups of thick dark coffee, smoke water pipes filled with Iranian tobacco, play chess and backgammon, and listen to a professional storyteller - the *naqqal* - recite episodes from Ferdowsi's *Shahnameh* with extravagant gestures and shifts of voice. Poetry was recited, gossip exchanged, deals struck.

The shahs watched the coffeehouses warily. They were places where men talked too freely, and where the boundary between political criticism and outright sedition was perilously thin. At various moments they were taxed, regulated, or briefly shut, but they always returned. Their descendants are still open on every Iranian street.

Wine, despite religious prohibition, was widely drunk, especially at the court and in aristocratic gardens. Shiraz was famous for its vintages long before any European had heard of Bordeaux. Shah Abbas held drinking parties that scandalized visiting clerics and delighted visiting ambassadors. Hashish and opium circulated too, the latter increasingly prevalent as the seventeenth century wore on.

Leisure, for those who could afford it, meant the garden. The Persian garden - *bagh* - was a paradise reduced to human scale, quartered by watercourses, shaded by plane trees, scented with jasmine and roses. Families picnicked in them, poets composed in them, lovers met in them. The Persian word *paradise*, after all, comes from the Old Persian *pairidaeza*, meaning "walled garden." Under the Safavids, that old vision was renewed and perfected, and a life of any comfort was measured in the hours a man or woman could spend inside one.

Festivals and the Public Display of Faith

The Safavid calendar was crowded with occasions on which the empire displayed itself to itself. Some were ancient, some new, and together they stitched the population into a shared rhythm of celebration and grief.

Nowruz, the Persian New Year at the spring equinox, was older than Islam and older than Zoroaster. The Safavids embraced it wholeheartedly. For thirteen days the empire paused. Families visited elders, settled quarrels, laid out the *haft-sin* table of seven symbolic foods beginning with the letter *s*, and wore new clothes. The shah held audiences, gave gifts, and received poets reciting panegyrics. Village and palace observed the same festival on the same day. Nowruz was, more than anything the chancery in Isfahan produced, the real unifier of Iranian identity.

If Nowruz was joy, Muharram was grief, and the Safavids made grief into a public act. The first ten days of the Islamic year commemorated the martyrdom of Imam Husayn at Karbala in 680 - the foundational tragedy of Shi'ite Islam. Under the Safavids, Muharram observances grew from subdued mourning into elaborate public spectacle. Men marched through the streets in black, beating their chests and, in more intense forms, striking themselves with chains. Preachers delivered *rawza* sermons that brought congregations to weeping. From the later seventeenth century, *ta'ziyeh*, passion plays reenacting the events of Karbala, developed into a distinctive Iranian theatrical form.

These processions were not only religious. They were political. Neighborhoods and guilds competed in the grandeur of their displays, and riots sometimes broke out between rival quarters. The Safavid state both encouraged these performances - they were, after all, advertisements for Shi'ism - and occasionally had to suppress their excesses.

Other occasions filled the year. The birthday of the hidden Twelfth Imam was celebrated with illuminations and charity. The anniversary of the martyrdom of Imam Ali, struck down in the mosque at Kufa, brought another round of mourning. Pilgrimages to Mashhad, Qom, Karbala, and Najaf drew tens of thousands every year, and the roads that served them were lined with caravanserais built by royal and private patrons.

Weddings, circumcisions, and royal births filled the streets with fireworks and free sweets; royal funerals filled them with professional mourners and black banners. When the shah returned from campaign, the city went out to meet him, carpets unrolled for miles along his approach, coins flung to the crowd.

The cumulative effect of all this, year after year and generation after generation, was to make Shi'ite Iran not merely a legal identity but a felt one. A child growing up in Isfahan in 1650 learned the Karbala story in the cradle, wept at Muharram from the age she could walk, exchanged Nowruz gifts with her cousins, and knew in her body what it meant to be a subject of the shah and a servant of the Imams. States rule by law; they endure by ritual.

Analysis

The Safavid political project - a Shi'ite Iran ruled from Isfahan - would ultimately fail in 1722, when Afghan invaders sacked the capital and ended the dynasty. But the social and cultural world described in these pages did not fail. It survived the fall of the empire almost intact. The bazaars kept their lanes, the villages their qanats, the nomads their pastures. The Nowruz table was still set in 1723. The Muharram processions still marched. The Armenian cathedrals of New Julfa still held Mass, and Zoroastrians in Yazd still tended their fires.

This was the Safavids' deepest achievement and their largest surprise. They set out to build a state, and they succeeded for two centuries. But what they built below the state, in the texture of daily life - a Persianate, Shi'ite, multi-ethnic civilization with its coffeehouses and its gardens, its hammams and its harems, its poets in the bazaar and its mothers in the shrine - outlasted everything. When modern Iran began in the twentieth century to ask who it was, it reached back, almost without knowing, to the world the Safavids had made.

Quick Summary

- Safavid society was a patchwork of cities, villages, and nomadic tribes, economically interdependent but culturally distinct.

- Women held defined legal rights and were powerful within the home; the royal harem became a major political force after Shah Abbas's seclusion reforms.

- Armenians, Jews, Zoroastrians, and Sunni Muslims all lived under Shi'ite rule with varying degrees of toleration, pressure, and forced conversion.

- Shah Abbas's deportation of Armenians to New Julfa in 1604-1605 created one of the great commercial diasporas of early modern Eurasia.

- Coffeehouses, introduced in the early seventeenth century, became central to male urban leisure and a source of official anxiety.

- Nowruz preserved pre-Islamic Iranian identity, while Muharram processions forged a distinctively Shi'ite public culture.

- Ta'ziyeh passion plays emerged as a unique Iranian theatrical tradition under late Safavid patronage.

- The daily and ritual life the Safavids shaped outlasted the dynasty itself and became foundational to modern Iranian identity.

A dynasty's monuments are easy to count - the mosques, the palaces, the manuscripts in the great libraries. Its true legacy is harder to see, because it is what people simply do. When an Iranian family today sets out the haft-sin at Nowruz, or mourns in black during Muharram, or drinks tea from a small glass in a teahouse where a storyteller once held forth, they are moving in grooves worn smooth by Safavid hands. The Crimson Crown fell in 1722. The civilization beneath it has not.

The rhythms of daily life ran on in streets and kitchens and teahouses, but they did not run unobserved. Safavid Iran was, for Europeans, one of the most visited cities outside their own continent, and the notebooks those visitors filled have become one of the richest sources we have for understanding how the empire felt from inside. The same processions Thomas Herbert watched in 1617 would be described, sketched, and argued over by friars, adventurers, jewelers, and diplomats for a century and a half. They came for silk, souls, stones, and alliances. Many of them stayed to write.

Chapter 14:

Strangers at the Gate

In the spring of 1598, an Englishman with questionable credentials and grander ambitions rode into the Safavid court. He carried no letter from his queen. He had no official standing. Within months, he would be helping to redesign the Iranian army.

His name was Anthony Shirley, and he was only the first of a remarkable parade. Over the next century and a half, Isfahan became one of the most visited, described, and argued-over cities in the world outside Europe. Carmelite friars in rough habits, English adventurers trailing debts across three continents, a French jeweler who would cross Iran six times, a Roman aristocrat escorting the embalmed body of his wife, Russian envoys bearing furs, Mughal ambassadors bearing elephants - all of them found their way to the Safavid capital. They left behind journals, letters, engravings, and polished memoirs that together form the richest eyewitness archive of any early modern empire east of the Mediterranean. Without these strangers, much of what we know about Safavid Iran would be rumor. With them, we can almost walk the streets of Shah Abbas's capital. But the view was never innocent.

The Sherley Brothers and the European Embassies

Anthony Shirley - the family spelled it several ways - was the sort of man the late Elizabethan age produced in abundance and tolerated with difficulty. Well-born, charming, chronically broke, and touched by a faint whiff of treason, he had drifted through service in the Netherlands, piracy in the Atlantic, and failed ventures in the Mediterranean before convincing a small band of followers that their fortunes lay in Persia. He arrived at Shah Abbas's court in 1598, a full two years before Queen Elizabeth signed the charter of the East India

Company. He had no instructions from London because London had not sent him.

None of that mattered to Abbas. The shah was then in the middle of the most daring project of his reign: breaking the power of the tribal Qizilbash cavalry that had put his dynasty on the throne and rebuilding his army around infantry, artillery, and a standing household force loyal only to him. Anthony Shirley and his younger brother Robert, who remained in Iran when Anthony departed as the shah's envoy to Europe, arrived with exactly the expertise that plan required. They knew European gunnery. They knew the drill of musketeers. They knew, or claimed to know, the courts of Christendom.

Robert Shirley stayed for nearly a decade, married a Circassian Christian noblewoman named Teresa, and by the time the Venetian traveler Pietro della Valle met him in 1619 was being credited - perhaps too generously - with the creation of a new corps of Safavid musketeers. Abbas, meanwhile, used Anthony to pursue a diplomatic fantasy: a grand Christian-Shi'a alliance against the Ottoman Sultan.

From 1603 and 1604 onward, the shah dispatched a series of embassies to the courts of Europe. Some were led by Iranians, some by the Shirleys, some by opportunistic Armenian merchants pressed into service. They travelled to Prague, Madrid, Rome, Warsaw, and eventually London, bearing letters in Persian, offers of commercial privilege, and a single insistent proposal: attack the Ottomans from the west while we attack them from the east. Every European monarch smiled, accepted the gifts, and did nothing. The Habsburgs had their own truces to manage; the English were more interested in silk than in crusades; the Pope blessed the messengers and filed the letters away.

The embassies failed on their own terms. Yet they succeeded in something the shah had not quite intended. They placed Iran on the mental map of European statecraft for the first time since the Mongols. Painters in Rome depicted Robert Shirley in a turban and gold brocade; the pamphlet presses of London printed breathless accounts of "the

Great Sophy." A Persian embassy in a European capital was news. It made the Safavid state legible, and therefore thinkable, to a continent that had previously lumped it together with every other Muslim power east of Vienna.

The Shirleys themselves ended badly, as such men usually do. Anthony died in obscurity in Madrid, pensioned but half-forgotten. Robert, after a second embassy to England, returned to Iran in 1628 and died at Qazvin the following year, his credit with Abbas exhausted. Teresa outlived them all and is buried in Rome. What survived them was a template - the European adventurer as unofficial intermediary - that others would soon fill with more talent and more pages.

Pietro della Valle, Tavernier, and Chardin

Pietro della Valle came to Iran not for trade, nor for diplomacy, nor for God, but for grief. A Roman nobleman whose beloved had recently refused him, he had vowed in 1614 to undertake a pilgrimage of such extravagant length that the pain might be worn out by the distance. He sailed to Constantinople, crossed to the Holy Land, visited Egypt and Mesopotamia, and in 1617 entered the domains of Shah Abbas. He would stay in the Safavid lands for more than five years.

Della Valle wrote letters home - very long letters. When they were eventually gathered and published, they ran to many volumes and became the single most influential European account of Iran in the seventeenth century. He met Abbas repeatedly, campaigned with him against the Ottomans in the Caucasus, and described the shah with a mixture of admiration and shrewdness that no European had managed before. Abbas was, by della Valle's account, informal, curious, ruthless, and disarmingly direct - a monarch who would drink with you, interrogate you about European artillery, and have a provincial governor blinded before breakfast. Along the way della Valle fell in love again, married a Chaldean Christian woman named Sitti Maani, and when she died in Iran preserved her body in order to bury her eventually in Rome. He carried her with him for years. That fact tells us more about early modern sensibility than any treatise.

Where della Valle offered sensibility, Jean-Baptiste Tavernier offered inventory. The son of an Antwerp map-seller turned jewel merchant, Tavernier crossed Iran six times between the 1630s and the 1660s on his way to and from the Mughal diamond mines. He was not interested in the soul of the East. He was interested in caravanserais, customs duties, the quality of pack animals, the going rate for a bale of silk at Tabriz, and above all stones. The Tavernier Blue, which he sold to Louis XIV, would eventually be recut and reborn as the Hope Diamond. His *Six Voyages*, published in 1676, reads like a merchant's ledger enlivened by gossip. It is, for exactly that reason, one of the most valuable economic documents we have for the period. Tavernier counted things. He told us what a road from Isfahan to Shiraz cost, in practice, to travel.

And then there was Jean Chardin. If della Valle was the poet of Safavid Iran and Tavernier its accountant, Chardin was its anatomist. A Huguenot jeweler from Paris, he made two long stays in Iran, the second lasting from 1673 to 1677, much of it in Isfahan under Shah Sulayman. He learned Persian. He read the chronicles. He attended court ceremonies, interviewed officials, inspected the royal workshops, and asked questions about the coinage, the provinces, the clergy, the women's quarters, and the succession. When persecution of French Protestants made return to France impossible, Chardin settled in London, was knighted by Charles II, and spent the rest of his life editing the ten volumes of his *Voyages en Perse*.

The result, published in stages from 1686 onward, is still the book scholars turn to first. Montesquieu mined it for the *Persian Letters*. Gibbon cited it. Modern historians of the Safavid bureaucracy still test their hypotheses against Chardin's descriptions. He got things wrong - he was, after all, a European gentleman working through informants of varying reliability - but he got an astonishing amount right, and he wrote with a calm, attentive curiosity that neither romanticized Iran nor condescended to it. He noted its decline as he saw it, admired its craftsmanship, criticized its theology, and loved Isfahan.

These three men - a heartbroken Roman, a Parisian gem dealer, and a Huguenot exile - between them defined what Europe knew about Iran for two hundred years. Their books were still being reprinted and read when Napoleon's envoys began to study the country for their own purposes.

Catholic Missionaries and the Politics of Religion

Alongside the adventurers and merchants came the friars. Shah Abbas, pursuing his anti-Ottoman alliance, had invited Catholic missionaries into his realm as a gesture of goodwill to the European courts he hoped to court. In 1607 a party of Portuguese Augustinians settled at Isfahan. Soon after came the Discalced Carmelites, dispatched by Pope Clement VIII, who established a permanent mission in the capital that would endure, remarkably, for over a century.

What the friars found was not what they had been led to expect. Iran was not a blank confessional field awaiting conversion. It was a Shi'a state with a self-confident clerical establishment, a small but ancient indigenous Christian community - the Armenians of New Julfa, just across the river from Isfahan - and a shah who had absolutely no intention of becoming a Catholic. Abbas was happy to host the friars, attend their Easter processions, tease them theologically, and use their presence as evidence to his European correspondents of his tolerant cosmopolitanism. He was not, despite the occasional hopeful rumor that reached Rome, on the verge of baptism.

The Carmelites adapted. Unable to convert Muslims, which was a capital matter in Iran as in every other Muslim state, they ministered to European residents, to merchant travelers passing through, and above all to the Armenians - whom they hoped to draw from their apostolic Church into union with Rome. This competition for Armenian souls produced decades of diplomatic friction with the Armenian archbishops of New Julfa, who held their own privileges from the shah and resented Latin poaching.

Yet the friars proved invaluable in ways no one had foreseen. They learned Persian. They wrote dictionaries. They kept chronicles of events at court. The Carmelite archive, preserved in Rome, is today a priceless source for the reigns of the later Safavids, describing palace intrigues and provincial revolts in the matter-of-fact tone of men who had been watching for a long time. They served as interpreters for visiting European embassies and sometimes as informal postmen carrying letters between Isfahan and the Mediterranean. They became, in effect, a permanent European listening post in the Safavid capital.

The religious politics were subtler than the missionaries themselves grasped. Abbas and his successors used Catholic presence to signal openness to Europe while losing nothing at home, because Iranian Muslims were essentially off-limits to the friars. Meanwhile the Shi'a clerical class, increasingly influential under the later shahs, watched the Europeans with suspicion and waited. Under Shah Sultan Husayn at the turn of the eighteenth century, that suspicion hardened into policy, and the space granted to Christians and other minorities shrank sharply. The friars' century of relative freedom had always been a gift of the crown, not a right.

Mughal Diplomacy and the Eastern Frontier

European visitors loom disproportionately large in our picture of Safavid Iran because Europeans wrote the books we now read. But for the Safavids themselves, the most consequential foreign power was not England or France or even the Papal States. It was the Mughal Empire, lying just beyond the Hindu Kush, with a population and revenue that dwarfed Iran's.

Relations between the two Persianate empires were ancient, literary, and prickly. The Mughal dynasty had been founded in 1526 by Babur, a Central Asian prince who wrote his memoirs in Turkish and thought of Persian as the language of high culture. When Babur's son Humayun was driven from India in 1540, he had fled to the Safavid court of Shah Tahmasp, who restored him to his throne at the price of public conversion to Shi'ism and a humbling diplomatic ceremony. Humayun returned to India; his Shi'ism quietly lapsed; and the memory of the debt, and the humiliation, shaped Mughal-Safavid relations for the next two centuries.

Qandahar was the flashpoint. This fortified city on the road between Iran and India was the gate to each empire from the other, and it changed hands repeatedly. Shah Abbas took it in 1622, exploiting Mughal preoccupation elsewhere. Shah Jahan recovered it in 1638 when its Safavid governor defected. Shah Abbas II took it back in 1649, and three Mughal expeditions failed to dislodge him. Behind each campaign lay tens of thousands of men, vast sums in treasure, and correspondence between the two courts that was elaborately courteous and murderously competitive.

The embassies sent back and forth between Isfahan and Agra, and later Delhi, are among the most spectacular of the early modern world. Mughal envoys arrived in Iran with elephants, jeweled swords, Kashmiri shawls, and poets. Safavid envoys went east with Arabian horses, Isfahan carpets, illuminated manuscripts, and their own poets. The two courts exchanged copies of the *Shahnama*, albums of miniatures, and carefully calibrated insults wrapped in flowery verse. Persian was the diplomatic language on both sides. A talented Iranian poet or calligrapher or physician could find greater patronage in Mughal India than at home, and many did: a steady eastward brain drain that enriched Indian culture and quietly weakened Iranian.

There were also Uzbek khans to the northeast, Russian tsars to the north, Ottoman sultans to the west, and a scatter of smaller Caucasian principalities paying tribute in one direction or another depending on the season. The Safavid foreign ministry, such as it was, had to manage all of them simultaneously. When European visitors marveled at

Isfahan's cosmopolitanism - Indian merchants, Russian envoys, Armenian silk traders, Arab scholars, Georgian pages, Turkish-speaking soldiers - they were seeing not an exotic spectacle but the normal working condition of an empire at the crossroads of Asia.

What the Outsiders Saw and What They Missed

European travelers gave us Isfahan in detail no Iranian chronicler ever attempted. They measured the squares and counted the shops in the bazaars. They described the tiles of the Shah Mosque, the polo games on the Maidan, the coffee houses where dervishes and merchants argued, the silk caravans arriving from the Caspian. They told us what the shah wore, what he ate, and how he laughed. They preserved voices and textures that would otherwise be lost.

But they also misread much of what they saw, and the misreadings are instructive. They consistently overstated the role of Europeans - Anthony Shirley did not single-handedly modernize the Safavid army, whatever his brother's publicists claimed; the reforms were Abbas's, drawing on Ottoman, Iranian, and European models alike. They underestimated the clerical establishment, perhaps because most travelers dealt with court officials and merchants and rarely entered the world of the madrasas. They treated Iran as essentially static, a land of immemorial custom, when in fact Safavid society was changing under their feet - its military reorganized, its capital rebuilt, its economy reoriented toward silk exports, its religious identity hardening into an increasingly assertive Shi'ism that would outlast the dynasty itself.

They saw the shah and missed the ulama. They saw the bazaar and missed the village. They saw Isfahan and too easily took it for Iran. And they wrote, inevitably, for European readers, which meant framing what they observed against European reference points - comparing the Maidan to St. Mark's Square, the Shi'a clergy to the Catholic hierarchy, the shah's absolutism to that of Louis XIV. Something always survives the translation. Something else is always lost.

Modern historians of Safavid Iran therefore use the European accounts the way a detective uses witness testimony: gratefully, and with care. Della Valle, Tavernier, Chardin, the Carmelite chronicles, the letters of the Shirleys - these are indispensable. They are also partial, interested, and sometimes self-serving. Read alongside Persian chronicles, administrative manuals, waqf deeds, and the archaeological record of Isfahan itself, they help us reconstruct a world. Read alone, they offer a brilliantly lit stage with most of the country hidden in the wings.

Key Figures & Events

Anthony Shirley's arrival in 1598 and the embassies he and his brother Robert carried to Europe in the early seventeenth century opened a channel of direct Iranian-European diplomacy for the first time in generations. Pietro della Valle's residence from 1617 to 1623 produced the first great literary account of Safavid Iran. Jean-Baptiste Tavernier's six voyages across the middle decades of the seventeenth century produced the definitive commercial survey, and Jean Chardin's second stay, from 1673 to 1677, yielded the encyclopedic *Voyages en Perse* that shaped European understanding of Iran for the next two centuries. The Carmelite mission, established at Isfahan after 1607, became a permanent European presence and a priceless archival source. On the eastern frontier, the long contest over Qandahar - lost in 1622, recovered by the Mughals in 1638, retaken by Iran in 1649 - defined Safavid-Mughal relations across three reigns.

Analysis

The Safavid century of openness to foreign visitors was not a triumph of tolerance or a sign of weakness. It was a policy. Shah Abbas and his successors used foreigners as they used everything else at their disposal - strategically. European adventurers brought military expertise. European merchants bought silk and paid in silver. European friars supplied diplomatic cover for anti-Ottoman alliances that never quite materialized. Mughal embassies confirmed Iran's standing in the Persianate world. Armenian, Indian, and Russian traders moved the goods that paid the taxes that funded the army. None of this was accidental. The Safavid state was, in its heyday, one of the most skillfully cosmopolitan regimes of the early modern world.

The accounts the foreigners wrote outlasted the state they described. When the Safavid dynasty fell in 1722 to an Afghan invasion, the European reading public already possessed a richer archive of Safavid Iran than of almost any non-European empire. That archive shaped, and sometimes distorted, how later generations - scholars, diplomats, colonial administrators, travelers - imagined the country. Iran in the European mind has always been partly Chardin's Iran, frozen on his carefully engraved pages. The strangers at the gate became, in the end, the storytellers whose version we still quote.

Quick Summary

- Anthony and Robert Shirley arrived in Iran from 1598, helping Shah Abbas modernize parts of his army and carrying his embassies to European courts.

- Shah Abbas's diplomatic push from 1603-04 sought, unsuccessfully, a Christian-Shi'a alliance against the Ottomans but placed Safavid Iran on Europe's political map.

- Pietro della Valle (resident 1617-23), Jean-Baptiste Tavernier (six voyages), and Jean Chardin (two stays, 1673-77) wrote the three most influential European accounts of Safavid Iran.

- Catholic missionaries, especially the Discalced Carmelites at Isfahan from 1607, maintained a permanent European presence and produced invaluable chronicles.

- The Mughal Empire, not any European state, was the Safavids' most consequential foreign counterpart, with Qandahar changing hands repeatedly between 1622 and 1649.

- Isfahan's cosmopolitan population reflected deliberate Safavid strategy, not accident.

- European accounts overstated European influence and underestimated the Shi'a clerical establishment whose power would outlast the dynasty.

The travelers came seeking silk, souls, stones, and alliances. They found an empire that used them at least as skillfully as they imagined they were using it. And when the Safavid state eventually collapsed, what remained of its daily life - the smell of its bazaars, the color of its tiles, the gossip of its court - survived largely in the notebooks of strangers. It is a strange fate for any civilization to be remembered most vividly through the eyes of visitors. Stranger still when those visitors got so much, and so little, right.

The travelers got much right and much wrong, but the empire they described was still, in their time, working. What they could not see from the audience halls and caravanserais was the quiet machinery of decay already turning inside the palace. Abbas the Great, the very shah whose reforms had made Iran safe enough to welcome Englishmen and Carmelites, had designed a system for protecting his throne from his own sons that would, within a century, hollow the dynasty from within. The princes who should have been learning to rule were instead being raised in a gilded prison, and the cost of that prison would eventually come due.

Chapter 15:

The Cage and the Crown

Shah Abbas the Great, architect of Iran's golden age, left behind a poisoned chalice. He had murdered one son and blinded two others, and he had locked his grandsons away in a gilded prison from which they would emerge, decades later, knowing nothing of the world they were expected to rule.

The system Abbas devised to protect his throne would, within a century of his death, destroy it. Safavid princes who had once been sent to govern provinces - learning horsemanship, administration, the management of warlords and tax collectors - were now confined to the harem among eunuchs and women. When their turn came to rule, they stepped from the shadows of the *haramsara* into the blinding light of kingship wholly unprepared. Some discovered a taste for wine and cruelty. Others retreated into ceremony. None matched the grandfathers who had built the empire they inherited. Four shahs across nearly a century each presided over a court more opulent and a state more hollow than the last. By the time an Afghan army appeared before Isfahan in 1722, the rot had been decades in the making, and its origins lay not in battlefield defeat but in a decision taken by the greatest Safavid of them all.

The Murder of Prince Safi Mirza

Abbas I had loved his eldest son. That, at least, is what the chroniclers tell us, and the terrible nature of what followed suggests they were right. Safi Mirza was handsome, accomplished, popular with the Qizilbash, a capable soldier. He was also, by the last years of his father's reign, the focus of every whisper at court about who would rule next.

That was enough to kill him. Abbas had spent his reign methodically neutralizing rivals - Qizilbash chieftains, Georgian and Circassian favorites who grew too powerful, even his own kinsmen. He trusted nobody, and as he aged his suspicions curdled into something closer to paranoia. When rumors reached him in 1615 that Safi Mirza was planning to seize the throne, he did not investigate. He acted.

A Circassian assassin was dispatched to Resht. Safi Mirza was cut down in a bathhouse, unarmed, almost certainly innocent of any plot. He was the heir Abbas had groomed, the son Persian poets had praised, and now he was a corpse in a provincial town. The grief that followed was operatic. Abbas is said to have wept, raged, ordered the executioner killed, and never quite recovered from what he had done.

The lesson he drew from this was not that he had been wrong. The lesson was that princes were dangerous. His two surviving sons, Khodabandeh Mirza and Imam Quli Mirza, were both blinded on his orders when similar suspicions crossed his mind - blinded because Islamic tradition held that a mutilated man could not rule, and therefore could not be a threat. A blind prince was a safe prince.

When Abbas died in 1629, there was no adult heir. The crown passed to his grandson, a teenager named Sam Mirza, the son of the murdered Safi Mirza. The boy took his father's name as his regnal title - Shah Safi I - a gesture either of mourning or of warning.

He had been raised in the harem. He had never commanded troops, administered a province, or sat in a council of state. What he had seen, from infancy, was the violent deaths of men connected to the throne. He was seventeen, and by the standards his grandfather had established, he was already a survivor.

The precedent now calcified into a rule. Safavid princes would no longer be sent to govern Khorasan or Fars to learn the craft of rule. They would be kept in the harem, under the eye of eunuchs and royal women, so that they could not plot and could not be plotted with. It was a system designed to produce safe heirs. It produced, instead, unfit ones.

Safi I and the Squandered Inheritance

Safi I began his reign as he meant to go on: with a purge. Within months of his coronation he had executed his grandfather's most trusted ministers, the generals who had won the great victories against the Ottomans, the women of the harem who might influence him, even members of his own family. The historian Iskandar Beg Munshi, who had chronicled Abbas I's glories, watched his patrons disappear one by one. The killing was so indiscriminate that it alarmed ambassadors and terrified the bureaucracy.

Some of this was paranoia inherited from his grandfather. Some of it was fear - the fear of a seventeen-year-old who had grown up watching men die and who assumed that any strong figure near the throne was a future assassin. Whatever its source, the result was the evisceration of the Safavid high command at the precise moment the empire needed it most.

The Ottomans noticed. In 1638, Sultan Murad IV marched on Baghdad, the great Mesopotamian city Abbas I had captured in 1623. Safi's army, stripped of competent commanders, could not relieve the siege. Baghdad fell. With it went the shrines of the Shia imams at Najaf and Karbala, the spiritual heartland of the faith the Safavids had made their own. The Treaty of Zuhab in 1639 fixed a border between Iran and the Ottoman lands that would, in its essentials, endure until the twentieth century. It also ratified the loss. Iraq was gone.

At home, Safi drank. He drank with a dedication that impressed even his courtiers, men accustomed to royal excess. Wine and opium filled the hours he might have spent on government. He executed men in fits of temper and regretted it in the morning. Chardin, the French jeweler who would later produce one of the greatest European accounts of

Safavid Iran, heard stories about Safi from men who had served him and recorded them with a kind of horrified fascination.

Yet the empire did not collapse. It did not collapse because of one man: Mirza Muhammad Taqi, known as Saru Taqi, the grand vizier. Saru Taqi was a eunuch, a castrated administrator whose very inability to found a dynasty made him trustworthy to the throne. He had risen under Abbas I as an honest provincial governor in a system famous for its corruption. Under Safi, he became indispensable.

Saru Taqi did the work of governing while the shah drank. He reorganized the treasury, crushed corruption in the provinces, converted Qizilbash tribal lands into crown domains that paid taxes directly to Isfahan, and kept the bureaucracy functioning through sheer force of will. He was, by all accounts, austere, incorruptible, and utterly fearless. He was also, eventually, murdered - in 1645, during the next reign - by a Qizilbash faction that resented his reforms.

Safi I died in 1642, at the age of thirty, his liver destroyed. He left an empire smaller than the one he had inherited, a bureaucracy kept alive by one remarkable vizier, and a nine-year-old son. The boy was crowned as Abbas II. For the second time in two reigns, a Safavid shah ascended the throne who had never governed anything, never commanded anyone, and never left the harem except to be told he was now the king of kings.

Abbas II: A Brief Restoration

Abbas II is one of the more surprising figures in Safavid history. By rights he should have been another Safi - a harem-raised boy dropped onto a throne he could not fill. Instead, for a while, he grew into something like the grandfather whose name he bore.

He was nine when he was crowned in 1642. For the first years of his reign, the real power lay with Saru Taqi, the vizier who had kept the state alive under his father. When Saru Taqi was murdered in 1645, the twelve-year-old shah surprised everyone by having the assassins executed in turn and appointing a new vizier, Khalifeh Sultan, a distinguished Shia scholar who restored order and continued the reforms. A boy of twelve, raised in the harem, had survived a vizierial coup without losing his throne. It was the first sign that Abbas II might be different.

As he grew, he took the business of ruling seriously. He held court, listened to petitions, travelled through his provinces, and made sure his generals knew he was watching. In 1649 he moved against the Mughals and retook Kandahar, the great fortress-city on the Afghan frontier that Abbas I had captured and Safi I had lost. When Shah Jahan's armies marched to retake it, they failed - three times. For a generation the Mughals had bullied the Safavid frontier. Abbas II bloodied their nose and held the line.

Inside his empire he practiced a kind of careful tolerance. He reversed his father's harsher measures against Armenian Christians and Jews, restoring the privileges the community in New Julfa had enjoyed under his great-grandfather. European visitors - Chardin arrived during his reign, and the Dutch and English trading companies found themselves welcome - described a court that was magnificent, ordered, and confident. Isfahan under Abbas II was perhaps the most cosmopolitan city west of Delhi.

It did not last. The shah had inherited his father's weakness for wine, and to wine he added other pleasures: women, young men, and, in the end, the slow poison of disease. Syphilis and throat cancer - the contemporary chronicles agree on the second, and most modern historians accept the first - wasted him through his twenties and early thirties. By 1666 he was unable to speak above a whisper. He died in October of that year. He was thirty-four.

His reign is often called a restoration, and it was - in the sense that a patient can be said to rally before dying. The institutions of the state worked. The armies won. The coinage was sound. But the structural problems Abbas I had bequeathed remained. The harem still produced the heirs. Princes still arrived on the throne without experience. When Abbas II's eldest son was brought out of the harem to be crowned, it became clear that the restoration had been personal, not systemic. The shah had been the thing holding the empire together. The shah was dead.

Sulayman and the Pleasures of the Palace

The boy who emerged from the harem on 1 November 1666 to be crowned as Safi II was nineteen, sickly, frightened, and almost entirely unknown to his courtiers. He had spent his life among women and eunuchs. He had been taught, if he had been taught anything useful, by a grandmother and a handful of tutors. Now he was shah.

His first reign, as Safi II, was a disaster. Famine struck. Plague followed. Prices in Isfahan tripled. An earthquake damaged parts of the capital. Rumors spread that the coronation had been performed on an inauspicious day, that the stars themselves had rejected the new king. The court astrologers, ever flexible, proposed a solution: crown him again, with a new name, at a more favorable moment.

On 20 March 1668, at Nowruz, the Persian New Year, the ceremony was repeated. Mohammad Baqir Sabzavari, the Shaykh al-Islam of Isfahan, presided over both crownings. The shah took a new regnal name: Suleiman, after the biblical Solomon, a king associated with wisdom and prosperity. Whether the astrologers had been right, or whether the famine had simply run its course, conditions did improve. Suleiman would keep the name for the rest of his life.

He kept little else of substance. Having survived the terrors of his early reign, Suleiman retreated into the harem from which he had so reluctantly emerged. He ruled for twenty-eight years and rarely left the palace. He appeared at public ceremonies when absolutely necessary, then vanished back into the private apartments, where he spent his days drinking, watching performances, and entertaining his favorites. Foreign ambassadors complained that they could not get an audience.

Provincial governors complained that they could not get instructions. The bureaucracy ran itself, which is to say, it ran down.

Most striking about Suleiman's reign, read in the chronicles, is how little happened. No great wars. No great reforms. No great building projects. The Ottomans, distracted by Vienna and the long war with the Habsburgs, did not press the western frontier. The Mughals, under an ageing Aurangzeb, were bogged down in the Deccan. Iran enjoyed a peace that was really an absence - the absence of enemies capable of exploiting its weakness.

Suleiman is said to have remarked, on his deathbed in 1694, that his empire was in trouble and that his sons were unfit to save it. If the story is true, it is the only piece of political insight attributed to him in thirty years. He then named no heir, leaving the succession to the eunuchs of the harem, who chose the son they thought would be easiest to control. They chose correctly. His name was Sultan Husayn, and under him the empire would fall.

The Decay of Provincial Government

While the shahs drank in the palace, the provinces were quietly coming apart. The process was slow, undramatic, and nearly invisible to contemporaries, which is why the collapse when it came felt so sudden.

Abbas I had built a tax system that depended on royal attention. He had converted large tracts of Qizilbash tribal territory into *khasseh*, crown land, administered directly from Isfahan by appointed officials. The revenues fed the court, the new standing army of *ghulam* slave-soldiers, and the magnificent building programs. The system worked because Abbas watched it, moved around his empire, executed corrupt governors, and rewarded efficient ones. Remove the watchful shah and the system rotted.

Under Suleiman, governorships became commodities. Men bought them in Isfahan and traveled to their provinces determined to extract, in a year or two, several times what they had paid. They taxed peasants into flight. They shook down merchants. They sold justice. The *khasseh* lands, which had been the treasury's lifeline, produced less and less because the peasants who worked them fled to tribal territories where the tax collector could not follow.

The army decayed in parallel. The *ghulam* corps, the Georgian and Circassian slave-soldiers who had been Abbas I's elite, lost their coherence as the court stopped investing in their training and recruitment. The Qizilbash tribal levies, nominally still part of the military system, had drifted back to pastoral semi-independence on the fringes of the empire. When the Safavid state needed an army in the next reign, it would find that it had, in effect, forgotten how to assemble one.

Frontier regions drifted furthest. In the Caucasus, Georgian princes played Isfahan off against Istanbul and did much as they pleased. In Kurdistan, tribal confederations paid nominal tribute and ignored everything else. In Baluchistan and along the Afghan border, the writ of the shah faded to nothing. The Ghilzai Afghans around Kandahar - Sunni tribesmen whose Shia Safavid governor would, in the next reign, provoke them beyond endurance - were already, by the 1690s, barely governed at all.

Merchants felt the decay most directly. The great trade routes that had made Isfahan rich - the silk trade through the Caspian, the overland routes from India, the Persian Gulf ports - became less safe and less profitable as local officials extorted travelers and bandits filled the security vacuum. The Armenian merchants of New Julfa, who had carried Persian silk to Amsterdam and Acapulco, began quietly to diversify their bases, opening houses in Venice and Madras and Manila, spreading their risk as the empire that had sheltered them wobbled.

Analysis

The standard story of Safavid decline blames weak shahs and a corrupt court, and it is not wrong. But it underestimates how deeply the problem was structural. Abbas the Great had solved one problem - the threat of ambitious princes - by creating another: the guarantee that every future shah would be unprepared. The harem produced rulers who could not rule. A court dominated by eunuchs and royal women selected, from that pool of unprepared men, those easiest to dominate. A bureaucracy that had once answered to a working shah answered, increasingly, to nobody.

What held the empire together through the seventeenth century was not its own strength but its neighbors' distractions. The Ottomans fought in Europe. The Mughals fought in the Deccan. The Russians had not yet reached the Caspian in force. Europeans came to trade, not to conquer. Iran was granted, by accident of geography and timing, a long grace period in which to decay quietly.

That grace period ended in 1722, when a Ghilzai army no bigger than a large Safavid tax-collecting expedition would have been walked to Isfahan and ended two and a quarter centuries of Safavid rule. That defeat belongs to the next chapter. Its causes belong to this one.

Quick Summary

- Abbas I killed his eldest son Safi Mirza in 1615 and blinded his other two sons, establishing a pattern of fearing heirs.

- Princes were confined to the harem rather than sent to govern provinces, producing rulers with no experience of command.

- Safi I (r. 1629-1642) purged his grandfather's ministers, lost Baghdad to the Ottomans in 1638, and governed through drink while the vizier Saru Taqi held the state together.

- Abbas II (r. 1642-1666) briefly revived Safavid fortunes, retaking Kandahar from the Mughals and patronizing a cosmopolitan court in Isfahan before dying at 34.

- His son Safi II, after a disastrous first year, was re-crowned as Suleiman I in 1668 and withdrew into the palace for 28 years.

- Under Suleiman, provincial governors became tax-farming predators, the army decayed, and frontier regions drifted toward independence.

- The empire survived the seventeenth century largely because the Ottomans and Mughals were occupied elsewhere, not because of its own strength.

In the whispered court of Suleiman, in the extorted villages of Fars, in the deserted barracks of the *ghulam* regiments, the Afghan catastrophe of 1722 was already written. A system built to prevent princely rebellion had succeeded perfectly, and in its success had guaranteed that when a real threat finally appeared, no prince would know how to meet it.

A system built to prevent princely rebellion had succeeded perfectly, and in its success had guaranteed that when a real threat finally appeared, no prince would know how to meet it. The threat, when it came, did not arrive from the Ottomans or the Mughals, who had shaped Safavid anxieties for two centuries. It came from the eastern frontier, from Kandahar, from tribes the court in Isfahan had barely troubled to understand. In the autumn of 1722, after a six-month siege that reduced the capital to cannibalism, the great-great-great-grandson of Ismail walked out of his palace and handed his crown to an Afghan.

Chapter 16:

The Afghan Hammer

In the autumn of 1722, after a six-month siege that reduced Isfahan to cannibalism, Shah Sultan Husayn walked out of his palace and placed his crown on the head of a tribal chieftain from Kandahar. The greatest empire of the Persian-speaking world had fallen.

The collapse was not sudden. For more than two centuries the Safavids had ruled from the Oxus to the Euphrates, fashioning a Shi'a state so culturally dominant that it defined what it meant to be Iranian. Yet by the 1720s the dynasty had hollowed itself from within. Its shah was a gentle, prayerful man who preferred theology to governance. Its harem eunuchs and clerical hardliners ran the administration. Its frontier subjects - especially the Sunni Pashtuns of Kandahar - had been pushed past endurance by tax collectors and zealots. And when the blow finally came, it came not from the Ottomans or the Mughals but from a few thousand tribesmen on horseback, crossing a thousand miles of desert to take the richest city on the Silk Road. How an empire of millions was unmade by a provincial warlord with a grudge is among the strangest stories in the history of Asia. It is also a case study in how slow rot, not sudden violence, ends dynasties.

Sultan Husayn: The Pious and the Helpless

When Shah Sulayman died in 1694, the court eunuchs who gathered around his deathbed were given a choice between two sons. One was reputed to be sharp and cruel. The other, Sultan Husayn, was said to be kind, devout, and easily led. They chose the second.

It was a decision that suited everyone who mattered inside the palace, and no one who lived outside of it. Sultan Husayn, then twenty-six, had been raised in the sealed gardens of the harem, educated by tutors chosen for orthodoxy rather than acuity. He emerged blinking into the throne room with a reputation for piety so pronounced that courtiers nicknamed him *Yakhshidir* - "Very Well" - because those were the only words he reliably offered to any question of state. He signed documents he had not read. He delegated decisions he did not understand. When told that Russian envoys had arrived, he is said to have asked whether Russians were a kind of Christian.

This was not a stupid man, by all accounts. He was a scholarly one, deeply versed in Shi'a jurisprudence, genuinely moved by the rituals of Muharram, endlessly generous in almsgiving. But the qualities that made him a credit to a madrasa made him a catastrophe on a throne. He believed, sincerely, that the right response to bad news was additional prayer. He believed that astrologers could identify the auspicious hour to march an army. He believed that wine was the chief enemy of the realm, and in his first year he ordered every bottle in the royal cellars smashed in the palace courtyard - an act of piety that shocked the Georgian and Armenian soldiers whose loyalty depended on such small indulgences.

Into this vacuum stepped Mohammad Baqir Majlesi, the chief mullah of Isfahan and one of the most formidable clerics in Safavid history. Majlesi had spent decades compiling the monumental *Bihar al-Anwar*, an encyclopedia of Shi'a tradition that remains consulted today. He was a theologian of genuine erudition and a politician of ruthless instinct. Under Sultan Husayn, Majlesi became something close to a shadow sovereign. He drafted decrees. He chose governors. He pushed the young shah to crack down on Sufi orders, on philosophers, on wine-drinkers, on Jews, on Zoroastrians, and - most consequentially - on the Sunni populations along the empire's eastern edge.

Majlesi died in 1699, but his program continued under disciples who shared his instincts without his intellect. The shah's mother, the harem bureaucracy, and a rotating cast of viziers formed a governing faction united chiefly by a desire to keep the shah pliable and the treasury flowing into their own estates. Tax revenues from the provinces were diverted to court expenses. Military stipends went unpaid. The *qurchis*, the elite royal guard, dwindled through neglect. When foreign observers visited Isfahan, they noted its beauty and its torpor in the same breath. The French Jesuit Tadeusz Krusinski, who lived in the capital for two decades, called the court "a place where nothing is done, and everything is discussed at length."

It was, in short, the kind of regime that could survive almost indefinitely in peacetime, and not three weeks under serious pressure.

Religious Persecution on the Frontiers

That pressure originated in a policy rather than an accident. The Safavid state had always rested on a sectarian foundation. Shah Ismail had forged Iran as a Twelver Shi'a polity, and for two centuries that identity had been defended, negotiated, and sometimes softened at the borders where the empire met Sunni majorities. Under Sultan Husayn, the softening stopped.

The eastern provinces were the most delicate of these frontiers. Kandahar, Herat, and the tribal highlands between them were overwhelmingly Sunni, populated by Pashtun confederations - the Ghilzai and the Abdali foremost among them - whose loyalty to Isfahan had always been contingent. The Safavids ruled these regions through a light touch: local chieftains collected taxes, kept the peace, and in return enjoyed wide autonomy and the courtesy of not being lectured about their religion. It was an imperfect system, but it had held for generations.

In the first decade of the eighteenth century, this arrangement was dismantled. Clerical factions in Isfahan pressed for the aggressive conversion of Sunni subjects to Shi'ism. New governors dispatched to the east arrived with instructions to enforce orthodoxy, demolish Sunni shrines, close mosques that refused to curse the first three caliphs in the

Friday sermon, and extract fresh taxes to fund these same pious exercises. The most consequential of these appointments was Gurgin Khan, a Georgian prince who had converted to Christianity, then back to Islam, and whose loyalty to the shah was matched only by his contempt for the Pashtuns he now governed.

Gurgin arrived in Kandahar around 1704. He brought with him a Georgian garrison and a reputation for cruelty that preceded him. He confiscated property from prominent Ghilzai families. He intervened in tribal marriages. He is said to have taken Pashtun women into his household against their will, an insult calibrated to humiliate a society in which female honor was the highest of goods. Pashtun chieftains who complained were arrested. Those who resisted were executed. Those who bribed him sufficiently were allowed, temporarily, to be left alone.

Similar patterns repeated across the eastern marches. In Shirvan, in the Caucasus, Sunni Lezgins rose against Shi'a officials who had desecrated their mosques. In Balochistan, local chieftains stopped remitting taxes. In Khorasan, the Uzbeks resumed their ancient habit of raiding as far south as Mashhad. Even within the Iranian heartland, Christian Armenians and Zoroastrians faced new taxes, forced conversions, and the steady confiscation of their places of worship. By 1715, the Safavid empire had managed, through sheer administrative zeal, to turn every one of its confessional minorities into a potential insurgent.

The irony was that the Safavid founders had built their state by mobilizing religious enthusiasm. Ismail's Qizilbash had ridden into battle chanting his name. But revolutionary zeal, once institutionalized, curdles into bureaucratic cruelty. What had once been a tool of conquest became a tool of provincial extortion, enforced by officials who cared more about the revenue than the theology and by clerics who cared more about the theology than the consequences.

In Kandahar, the consequences were about to arrive in the person of a local notable named Mirwais Hotak. He had been to Isfahan. He had seen the weakness. He had prayed, in the forbidden Sunni fashion, at the tomb of the Prophet in Medina, and he had come home with a plan.

The Ghilzai Revolt in Kandahar

Mirwais Khan Hotak was, by background, exactly the kind of man the Safavid system had been designed to co-opt. He was the headman of the Ghilzai confederation's most prominent clan, wealthy from the caravan trade that ran between Kandahar and the Indian frontier, literate in Persian and Pashto, and politically shrewd enough to understand that direct confrontation with Isfahan was suicide. Gurgin Khan, who knew a rival when he saw one, had him arrested in 1707 and sent in chains to the Safavid capital.

This was a mistake. In Isfahan, Mirwais was not executed - Gurgin had hoped he would be - but placed under a kind of courtly house arrest, free to move about the capital, meet officials, attend audiences, and observe. What he observed astonished him. The shah was a cipher. The viziers bickered. The treasury was empty. The royal army existed largely on paper. The Georgian general who terrorized Kandahar had few friends at court and many enemies. Mirwais made careful notes of these enemies and befriended them.

He also made the hajj. Traveling from Isfahan to Mecca, he sought out leading Sunni scholars and obtained from them a formal *fatwa*: rebellion against a heretical Shi'a ruler was not only permitted but obligatory. Whether this document was as authoritative as Mirwais later claimed is impossible to know, but its existence, carried home in a saddlebag, gave religious sanction to what had until then been a personal grievance.

By 1709, Mirwais was back in Kandahar, restored to favor, and apparently reconciled with Gurgin Khan. He invited the governor and his senior officers to a hunting party outside the city. The afternoon went pleasantly. Wine was served. Gurgin, relaxed and poorly guarded, was cut down with his entire retinue. Mirwais rode back into Kandahar that night and declared the province free of Safavid rule.

Isfahan's response was a textbook illustration of how not to handle a rebellion. The first army sent against Mirwais, under a Safavid prince named Khusraw Khan, arrived in 1711 with thirty thousand men. It was badly supplied, badly led, and demoralized by the march. Mirwais drew it into a defensive siege of Kandahar, then sallied out with his lightly armed Ghilzai cavalry and annihilated it. Khusraw was killed. His army disintegrated. The survivors who straggled back to Isfahan reported what they had seen - an enemy that fought with ferocity, a countryside that supplied the rebels, a Safavid commissariat that had failed almost before the campaign began.

A second expedition in 1713 did no better. It reached Kandahar, found the walls strengthened, the population hostile, and its own supply lines impossibly long. It retreated in disorder, harried by Ghilzai horsemen for two hundred miles. After this second failure, the court in Isfahan made a decision that amounted to acquiescence. No third army was dispatched. Kandahar was, in practice, lost.

Mirwais ruled it as an independent emirate until his death in 1715. He never claimed the title of king, preferring the modest Pashtun honorific of *khan*, and he cultivated the pretense that he remained, technically, a loyal subject of the shah. It was a useful fiction for both sides. But he had trained his sons and nephews in a different understanding. He had taught them that the Safavid empire was a pyramid of brittle pretensions: touch it hard enough in the right place, and it would collapse.

After Mirwais died, a brief succession struggle brought his son Mahmud to power. Mahmud was eighteen, violent, intermittently deranged - contemporaries spoke of fits of paranoia and episodes of catatonic melancholy - and possessed of a conviction his father had lacked: that Kandahar was not the end of the Ghilzai ambition but the beginning.

Mahmud's March and the Battle of Gulnabad

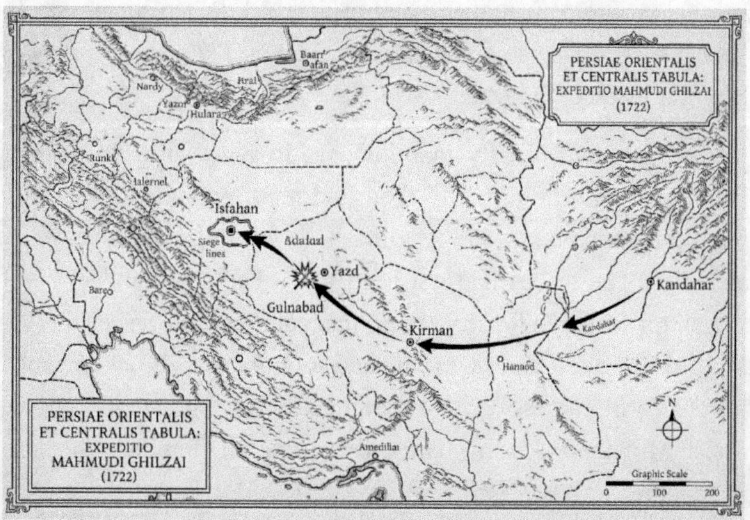

Mahmud's March and the Fall of Isfahan, 1722

Mahmud's first serious probe westward came in 1719, when he led a Ghilzai army across the Dasht-e Lut desert to the city of Kerman. He took it, held it briefly, plundered its markets, and withdrew. Isfahan noticed, then declined to respond. The shah's astrologers reportedly advised waiting for a more auspicious conjunction.

In the summer of 1721, Mahmud set out again, this time with a larger force - something between twenty and forty thousand, depending on which contemporary account one believes - and a clear objective. He meant to take Isfahan itself. It was an audacious plan bordering on the delusional. The Safavid capital was nine hundred miles from Kandahar across some of the most hostile terrain in Asia. It was walled,

189

provisioned, and in theory defended by an imperial army many times the size of Mahmud's. No invader had reached it from the east in living memory.

The march succeeded partly because the Safavids refused to believe it was happening. Reports from Kerman, Yazd, and Isfahan's own frontier garrisons were dismissed or delayed. When Mahmud's forces appeared outside the capital in early March 1722, the court was still debating whether the threat was real.

The army that finally marched out to meet him was, on paper, overwhelming. Perhaps fifty thousand men, with elephants, artillery, and the remnants of the Qizilbash cavalry. In practice it was a shambles. The troops had not been paid. The commanders had been chosen for factional loyalty rather than competence. The artillery train, dragged out of storage, was manned by gunners who had never fired the pieces in earnest. Overall command was entrusted to the Grand Vizier, Mohammad Qoli Khan, and to a council of nobles who despised one another.

They met the Afghans at Gulnabad, a village about twelve miles east of Isfahan, on the morning of March 8, 1722. What followed was less a battle than a demonstration. The Safavid right, under the Arab governor of the Persian Gulf, charged early and without coordination, was surrounded, and was cut to pieces. The center wavered. The left, commanded by a Georgian contingent, fought bravely and held its ground but found itself unsupported. The Safavid artillery fired a few rounds and was abandoned. The elephants, spooked by musketry, turned and trampled their own infantry. By early afternoon the Safavid army had ceased to exist as a fighting force. Between five and fifteen thousand imperial soldiers lay dead on the plain. Mahmud's losses were perhaps a tenth of that.

Gulnabad was not decisive in the sense of being a hard-fought field. It was decisive in the sense that it revealed, in a single morning, that the Safavid state could not defend itself. The emperor of half of Asia had staked everything on one battle, a dozen miles from his own palace, and had lost it to a tribal army less than half the size of his own.

The court, when the news arrived, responded with the paralysis that had become its characteristic mode. The shah wept. The mullahs called for additional prayers. Some courtiers urged flight; others urged negotiation; a few suggested arming the citizenry. None of these things were done with conviction. Mahmud's army, pausing only to consolidate its victory and plunder the abandoned Safavid camp, moved west and began to invest the capital.

The Siege and Fall of Isfahan

Isfahan in 1722 was one of the great cities of the world. Its population approached six hundred thousand. Its central square, the Naqsh-e Jahan, was the largest urban space in Asia. Its bazaars traded Gujarati indigo and Venetian glass. Its walls, though long and not uniformly strong, enclosed palaces, gardens, colleges, and the river Zayandeh Rud that watered the whole. Mahmud had perhaps twenty thousand men. He could not assault such a city. He could only surround it and wait.

He was helped by two Safavid failures. The first was strategic: no attempt was made, in the critical weeks after Gulnabad, to break Mahmud's siege from outside. Provincial governors sat on their forces and watched. Tahmasp, the shah's son and designated heir, escaped the city in June with a small retinue and rode north to Qazvin, supposedly to raise an army, but in practice to wait and see. The second failure was logistical: the capital had not been provisioned. Despite months of warning, granaries had not been filled. Within six weeks of the blockade beginning, prices in the bazaars had tripled. Within three months, they had risen tenfold.

What followed was among the worst urban famines of the early modern era. By July, residents were eating the city's horses, then its donkeys, then its dogs and cats. By August they were eating leather -

boiling saddles and boots into a kind of broth. By September they were eating the bark of trees and the bodies of those who had died of hunger. European missionaries inside the walls, including the Jesuit Krusinski and the Polish priest Pere Bazin, recorded what they saw with the flat disbelief of men attempting to preserve evidence. Parents ate children. The dead were sold in the markets. A loaf of bread, when it could be found, cost a gold coin. Whole districts of the city were simply emptied of the living.

Inside the palace, Sultan Husayn prayed. He also attempted, periodically, to negotiate. He offered Mahmud tribute. He offered him a provincial governorship. He offered him a Safavid princess in marriage. Mahmud, camped in the gardens of Farahabad just outside the walls, rejected each offer in turn. He now understood what his father had understood. He was not negotiating for a province. He was negotiating for an empire.

On October 21, 1722, after six and a half months of siege, Sultan Husayn surrendered. Accompanied by a small escort of courtiers - those still strong enough to walk - he rode out of the city to Mahmud's camp. There, in a ceremony whose details were recorded by multiple witnesses, the last effective Safavid shah dismounted, approached the Ghilzai chieftain, removed the aigrette-studded turban from his own head, and placed it on Mahmud's. He declared, according to one account, that God had transferred the kingdom from his house to Mahmud's, and that he accepted this judgment with the resignation of a believer.

Four days later, on October 25, Mahmud entered Isfahan. He did not, at first, sack it - the city had little left to sack. He installed himself in the royal palace, seated himself on the peacock throne, and began receiving the submissions of what remained of the Safavid nobility. He was twenty-four years old. He was the ruler of Iran.

Analysis

The fall of Isfahan was not, in any normal sense, a military defeat. Mahmud's army was small, poorly equipped, and operating at the end of an impossibly long supply line. A functioning empire would have destroyed it before it reached Kerman. The Safavid state in 1722 was not a functioning empire. It was a court, a clerical establishment, and a tax-collection apparatus, none of which were capable of projecting force beyond their own palace walls.

A deeper cause of the collapse was the transformation of Safavid ideology from a mobilizing myth into a persecuting bureaucracy. Ismail had used Shi'ism to conquer; Sultan Husayn used it to alienate. The Sunni frontier, which had been integrated through tolerance, was lost through zealotry. The Christian and Zoroastrian minorities, who had supplied soldiers and merchants, were turned into enemies. Even within the Shi'a majority, the domination of a narrow clerical faction suffocated the intellectual and economic energies that had once made Isfahan a world city.

A pattern recurs in the history of empires. Revolutionary movements succeed through the passion of their followers. They endure through the competence of their administrators. They collapse when the administrators, grown comfortable, redirect the original passion into the narrowest possible channels - into purity tests, factional patronage, and the harassment of the weak. The Safavid end was a textbook case. Mahmud's hammer fell on a structure that had already been eaten hollow from within.

Key Figures & Events

- **Sultan Husayn (r. 1694-1722):** Pious, indecisive last effective Safavid shah; surrendered Isfahan and was executed in 1727.

- **Mohammad Baqir Majlesi (d. 1699):** Senior cleric whose hardline policies shaped the persecution of non-Shi'a subjects.

- **Gurgin Khan:** Georgian governor of Kandahar whose cruelty toward the Ghilzai triggered rebellion; assassinated by Mirwais in 1709.

- **Mirwais Hotak (d. 1715):** Ghilzai chieftain who studied Safavid weakness in Isfahan and made Kandahar independent.

- **Mahmud Hotak (d. 1725):** Mirwais's son; won Gulnabad, took Isfahan, ruled as shah until his death.

- **Battle of Gulnabad (March 8, 1722):** Safavid imperial army routed by a much smaller Afghan force.

- **Siege of Isfahan (March-October 1722):** Six-month blockade produced famine, cannibalism, and surrender.

Quick Summary

- Sultan Husayn, a pious but ineffectual ruler, presided over two decades of administrative decay after 1694.

- Clerical policies aimed at converting Sunni frontier populations, especially Pashtuns, destabilized the eastern provinces.

- In Kandahar, the Georgian governor Gurgin Khan's brutality drove the Ghilzai chief Mirwais Hotak to revolt in 1709.

- Two Safavid expeditions against Kandahar failed disastrously, leaving the province effectively independent.

- Mirwais's son Mahmud captured Kerman in 1719 and marched on Isfahan in 1722.

- At Gulnabad on March 8, 1722, a small Afghan army destroyed a much larger Safavid force in a single morning.

- The ensuing six-month siege produced one of the worst urban famines of the early modern period.

- On October 21, 1722, Sultan Husayn surrendered and placed his crown on Mahmud's head, ending Safavid rule over Iran.

The Afghan occupation of Isfahan would prove short and unstable. Mahmud descended into paranoid massacres before his own cousin Ashraf replaced him in 1725. Tahmasp II, declared shah in Qazvin, would struggle to organize resistance from the north. Russian and Ottoman armies, sensing the vacuum, sliced off territories in the Caucasus and the west under the Treaty of Constantinople of 1724. Yet none of these powers would inherit Iran. That role would fall to an obscure Turcoman warlord from Khorasan, a former bandit and camel-driver named Nader, whose rise from the ruins of 1722 would constitute the final, and strangest, chapter of the Safavid story.

Mahmud's paranoid massacres, Ashraf's usurpation, the Russian and Ottoman carving of the frontiers: none of these would decide the shape of post-Safavid Iran. That role fell to someone the courts of 1722 had never heard of, an illiterate camel-driver from Khorasan whose genius for war would restore the empire's frontiers even as he drained it of what remained of its wealth. Nader Quli used the Safavid name as a ladder and, when he had climbed high enough, kicked it away. The fourteen years between the fall of Isfahan and his own coronation are the strangest chapter the dynasty ever lived through.

Chapter 17:

Twilight and Nadir

On a cold October morning in 1722, the last crowned shah of Isfahan walked out of his capital to surrender his turban to an Afghan warlord. The empire his great-great-great-grandfather Ismail had forged in blood and prophecy was, by any reasonable measure, finished. And yet the Safavid story had fourteen more strange years to run.

Those years belong less to the Safavids themselves than to the man who used their name as a ladder. Nadir Quli of the Afshar tribe - illiterate, brilliant, and ferociously cruel - restored Iran's frontiers in the name of a shah he kept in gilded captivity, then stepped across the empty throne to claim it for himself. The dynasty that had given Iran its faith, its borders, and much of its modern character did not die at Isfahan in 1722. It died at a dusty assembly on the Mughan steppe in 1736, killed off by the very general who had saved it. What followed was stranger still: pretenders bearing Safavid blood, or claiming to, kept surfacing for decades, ghosts in a country that could not quite let the dynasty go.

Tahmasp II and the Government in Exile

When the Afghan chieftain Mahmud Hotak took Isfahan, he did not take every Safavid prince. One young son of Shah Sultan Husayn slipped out of the city before the siege tightened and rode north. His name was Tahmasp, and he was about eighteen.

He fled to Qazvin, then, when the Afghans pushed after him, to Tabriz, then deeper still into the Caspian provinces. Along the way he did what any Safavid heir would do: he had himself proclaimed shah. Tahmasp II was a monarch with a court, a seal, and almost no country.

The Afghans held the centre. The Ottomans, sensing a carcass, had marched into the west and seized Hamadan, Kermanshah, and much of Azerbaijan. The Russians under Peter the Great had bitten off the Caspian coast. What remained of Iran was a scatter of provinces where local khans calculated, daily, which master would serve them best.

Tahmasp's government-in-exile was a curious thing. It had the trappings of Safavid sovereignty - the royal chancery, the Shi'a clerical blessing, coinage struck in the shah's name - but it depended entirely on whichever tribal commander agreed to host it. For a time that was the Qajars of Astarabad, old rivals of the dynasty who now found it useful to shelter its heir. For a time it was the Kurds. The young shah drank heavily, quarrelled with his advisors, and waited for a champion to arrive.

Later chroniclers, writing under Nadir, had every reason to portray Tahmasp as feckless and drunken, a husk of royalty waiting to be swept aside. Some of that is surely propaganda. But the essential picture holds: a young man raised in the stifling harem of late-Safavid Isfahan, suddenly thrust into a war he was not equipped to fight, clinging to legitimacy because legitimacy was all he had.

What he did possess was the name. In a country where the Safavid shah was still, in the minds of most Iranians, the shadow of God on earth - and in the minds of the Qizilbash tribes, a living saint descended from the Imams - that name was worth armies. It was only a question of who would come to claim it on his behalf.

The answer arrived in 1726, on horseback, from the east.

The Rise of Nadir Quli

He had been born Nadir Quli - "slave of the rare one" - in 1688, in the stony uplands of northern Khorasan. His people were Afshars, one of the original Qizilbash tribes that had put Ismail on the throne two centuries earlier. His family were herders, not nobles. As a boy he was reportedly carried off by Uzbek raiders and spent years in captivity before escaping. Whether true or embroidered, the story suited the man he became: self-made, scarred, unsentimental.

By his thirties Nadir was a local strongman in the district of Abivard, leading a band of cavalry, collecting tolls, fighting other warlords. Khorasan in the 1720s was a land without government, and such men thrived there. When Tahmasp II's wandering court came within reach, Nadir saw his opening. He presented himself in 1726 and offered his sword.

The shah accepted. He could hardly refuse. Nadir brought with him perhaps five thousand disciplined horsemen, more than any other commander in Tahmasp's service. In gratitude - and in a gesture that would haunt him - the shah gave Nadir a new name: Tahmasp Quli Khan, "the slave of Tahmasp." It was meant as an honour. Nadir would wear it like a mask until he chose to throw it off.

Within eighteen months Nadir had reorganised Tahmasp's scrappy forces into something like a modern army. He drilled his infantry in the use of the musket and light cannon, the weapons the Safavids had never taken seriously enough. He broke the power of rival warlords who had been milking the shah's court for patronage. He was ruthless with his own officers: a commander who failed might be blinded; one who disobeyed might be executed on the spot. Men who survived his discipline became fanatically loyal.

He also made himself, quietly, the real government. Tahmasp remained the shah, but every decision of consequence now ran through his Afshar general. When a rival commander, Fath Ali Khan Qajar, objected to Nadir's ascendancy, Nadir had him executed in the shah's own camp, on the shah's own orders, which the shah had been persuaded to sign. It was an early demonstration of how power would flow in this partnership.

Nadir was not, by the standards of his age, a cultivated ruler. He could barely sign his name. He had no interest in theology, poetry, or the elaborate ceremonial of Safavid kingship. What he had was a genius for logistics and a terrifying instinct for when to strike. Contemporaries who met him described a tall, dark, heavily built man with a voice that could carry across a battlefield and eyes that made grown courtiers look at the floor. He slept little, ate simply, and trusted almost no one.

In a country starved of competent leadership, such a man was bound to rise. The only question was how far.

Driving Out the Afghans and Ottomans

The first target was the Afghans. The Hotak dynasty that had taken Isfahan had already begun to fracture - Mahmud had gone mad and been murdered by his cousin Ashraf - but they still held the heart of Iran. In 1729 Nadir marched west at the head of an army that had, at last, caught up with the military revolutions of Europe and the Ottomans.

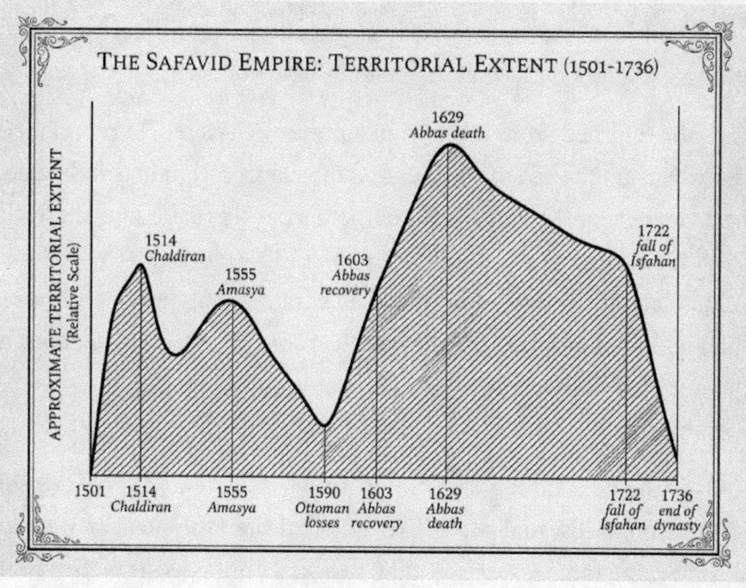

Safavid Territorial Extent, 1501–1736

He met Ashraf's forces at Damghan in September and broke them. He met them again at Murchakhort, just north of Isfahan, in November, and broke them for good. Ashraf fled toward Kandahar and was killed on the road. Nadir rode into Isfahan and restored Tahmasp II to the palace his family had lost seven years before. The citizens wept. The empty halls filled again with the smoke of Safavid ritual. For a moment it looked as though the old order had simply been interrupted.

It had not. With the Afghans crushed, Nadir turned west against the Ottomans, who still held Hamadan, Tabriz, and much of Azerbaijan. Here, too, he was largely successful. Through 1730 his armies recovered city after city. Tahmasp's restoration seemed complete.

Then Nadir gave Tahmasp the opportunity to make a serious mistake. Called away to suppress a revolt in Khorasan, he left the shah in nominal command of the western front. Tahmasp, hungry to prove himself a warrior in his own right, launched an offensive against the Ottomans in 1731. It was a disaster. He lost an army, lost the cities Nadir had just recovered, and was forced to sign a humiliating treaty ceding back much of what his general had won.

Nadir returned from the east in a controlled rage. He repudiated the treaty. He summoned the nobles and the clergy to Isfahan and presented the evidence of Tahmasp's incompetence - the drinking, the military folly, the unfitness to rule. In August 1732 Tahmasp II was deposed. In his place Nadir raised up the shah's infant son, barely eight months old, and had him proclaimed as Shah Abbas III. It was a naked power-play dressed in dynastic piety. The baby was a symbol; the regent was everything.

Over the next three years Nadir, ruling as regent, retook everything Tahmasp had lost and more. He defeated the Ottomans at Baghavard in 1735 and forced a peace that restored Iran's western frontier. He pushed the Russians out of the Caspian provinces by a mix of negotiation and menace. By the winter of 1735-36, Iran was whole again, within borders its people had not seen since the days of Shah

Abbas the Great. The man who had done this was thirty-seven years old, the guardian of a toddler, and manifestly the master of the realm.

The puppet was about to be put away.

The Mughan Assembly and the End of the Dynasty, 1736

In January 1736 Nadir summoned the grandees of Iran to an encampment on the Mughan steppe, in the flatlands south of the Aras River. Thousands came: khans of the tribes, governors of the provinces, Shi'a clerics, Sunni notables from the recovered territories, Armenian bishops, Georgian princes, merchants, soldiers. The tent city stretched for miles. It was the largest political gathering Iran had seen in living memory, and everyone understood why it had been called.

The script was carefully written. Nadir announced that he was weary, that he wished to retire to his estates, that the realm needed a strong hand and that he could no longer provide one while the true dynasty lived. He invited the assembly to choose a shah from the Safavid house. The assembly, understanding its part, begged him to take the throne himself. A few bold voices argued that the Safavids, however diminished, were the God-chosen line - but such voices were heard and then silenced. Nadir accepted with a show of reluctance, on conditions: that Iran abandon the excesses of Shi'a piety that had made it a pariah among its neighbours; that the curses against the first three caliphs be dropped; that a softer form of Shi'ism, acceptable to Sunni powers, become the state creed.

The religious concession was as radical as the dynastic one. For two and a half centuries, Safavid Iran had defined itself by its militant Twelver Shi'ism. Nadir proposed to fold that identity into a broader, blander Islam more useful to an empire-builder. The clerics at Mughan assented - some enthusiastically, most because the alternative was unspeakable. One senior mujtahid who opposed the plan was quietly strangled in his tent.

On 8 March 1736 - Nowruz, the Persian new year - Nadir was crowned shah of Iran. The Afsharid dynasty had begun. The Safavid dynasty, after two hundred and thirty-five years, was over.

What happened next was the part Nadir tried not to think about. Tahmasp II and his two small sons, including the child who had briefly been Shah Abbas III, were held as prisoners in Khorasan. For a few years they were kept alive, hostages against Safavid uprisings. In 1740, when Nadir's own son Reza Quli - acting on his own authority, or perhaps on a hint - ordered their execution, they were killed. The line of Shah Ismail, which had produced ten reigning monarchs and reshaped a civilisation, ended in a provincial garrison at the edge of a knife.

Nadir himself went on to sack Delhi in 1739 and carry off the Peacock Throne and the Koh-i-Noor diamond, becoming for a few years the richest conqueror on earth. He was assassinated by his own officers in 1747, having grown so paranoid he had ordered the blinding of his eldest son. His empire collapsed within weeks of his death. The Afsharids lasted a single generation.

Pretenders and Echoes Through the Eighteenth Century

The Safavids refused to stay buried. In the chaos that followed Nadir's murder, at least three pretenders surfaced claiming Safavid descent, each attracting followers among tribes and cities that remembered the old dynasty as a golden age. The most successful was Ismail III, a genuine grandson of Shah Sultan Husayn, raised to the throne in 1750 by the Bakhtiari chieftain Ali Mardan Khan and then by the far more capable Karim Khan Zand.

Karim Khan ruled most of Iran from Shiraz for nearly three decades, and he ruled well - peacefully, fairly, with an attention to commerce and ordinary life that his countrymen remembered with affection. But he never took the title of shah. He called himself *vakil*, the regent, the deputy. On his coins and in his edicts the sovereign was always a Safavid - first Ismail III, a harmless boy kept in comfortable confinement, and after his death simply the absent Safavid house in the abstract. Karim Khan understood what Nadir had tried to deny: that in the Iranian imagination, legitimate sovereignty still belonged to the family of Shah Ismail.

Other Safavid claimants rose and fell. One surfaced in Georgia, another in the Caucasus, a third among the Afghans. Some were fraudulent, some may have been genuine. All were eventually killed or bought off. When the Qajar Agha Muhammad Khan finally reunified Iran in the 1790s and crowned himself shah, he made a point of exterminating the last traceable male-line Safavids he could find. The dynasty had to be definitively extinguished before a rival one could plausibly take its place.

Even then, the ghost lingered. Nineteenth-century travellers in Iran reported peasants in remote valleys who still, when pressed, named the Safavids as the rightful line. The family had become less a political force than a memory of order, piety, and Iranian self-respect.

Analysis

What Nadir did at Mughan was, on its face, a straightforward usurpation: a general with an army took a crown from an infant who could not defend it. But the gesture was more revealing than that. Nadir had spent a decade restoring the Safavid realm, fighting in the Safavid name, winning battles under a Safavid flag. He understood, better than anyone, how much of Iran's recovery depended on that name. And still, when the moment came, he set it aside.

He did so because he believed - wrongly, as it turned out - that raw military success could manufacture a new legitimacy. It could not. His own dynasty fell apart the instant he died. The Zands who followed refused the title of shah out of respect for the ghost he had murdered. The Qajars who finally replaced the Zands spent their first decades

203

anxiously asserting, through marriages and ceremonies and carefully curated genealogies, that they were the rightful heirs to something - a something that was, inescapably, Safavid.

The Safavids had done what few dynasties anywhere have done: they had fused a faith, a language, a territory, and a political culture into a single thing called Iran. Killing the family did not unmake the fusion. It could not be unmade. That, in the end, is the measure of what Ismail had begun in 1501 and what Nadir, for all his brilliance, could not undo in 1736.

Quick Summary

- After Isfahan fell to the Afghans in 1722, Prince Tahmasp fled north and established a wandering government-in-exile as Tahmasp II.

- Nadir Quli, a brilliant Afshar tribal commander from Khorasan, joined Tahmasp's court in 1726 and quickly became the real power behind the throne.

- Nadir drove the Afghans out of Isfahan in 1729 and began reclaiming territory from the Ottomans in the west.

- In 1732, after Tahmasp II lost a disastrous campaign against the Ottomans, Nadir deposed him and installed the infant Shah Abbas III.

- At the Mughan assembly in March 1736, Nadir had himself crowned shah, ending the Safavid dynasty after 235 years.

- Tahmasp II and his sons, including the child Abbas III, were executed in 1740.

- Safavid pretenders reappeared for decades; Karim Khan Zand ruled as regent for a puppet Safavid until 1779, refusing the title of shah.

- The Qajars, who reunified Iran in the 1790s, systematically eliminated the last Safavid claimants.

The twilight of the Safavids lasted longer than anyone at the fall of Isfahan would have predicted, and its afterglow longer still. Nadir Shah believed he had closed the book on a spent dynasty and opened a new chapter under his own name. He was half right. The book was closed. But the language it had been written in - Shi'a, Persian, imperial, unmistakably Iranian - was the only language in which the next chapters could be composed. Every shah who followed, down to the last in 1979, ruled in a country the Safavids had made.

The book was closed, but the language remained. Every shah who followed Nader, down to the last in 1979, ruled in a country the Safavids had made: Shi'a, Persian, imperial, drawn on borders a teenage mystic had first sketched with cavalry. What exactly had been inherited, and by whom, is a question Iran has been answering ever since. The tilework on the domes of Isfahan, the rites in its mosques, the arguments in its seminaries, the very shape of its map - all of these outlived the dynasty that produced them, and all of them continue to do political work five centuries on.

Chapter 18:

The Safavid Inheritance

Walk through the center of Isfahan on a summer evening, and you are walking through a Safavid dream. The tiled domes still catch the last light. The square still holds the scale Shah Abbas intended. And the prayers murmured inside the Sheikh Lotfollah Mosque still follow the Twelver rite that Ismail imposed, at sword point, five centuries ago.

The dynasty that raised this city fell in 1736, crushed by Afghan invaders and finished off by the ambitions of Nader Shah. Yet of all the empires that rose and collapsed across early modern Eurasia, few left an inheritance so thoroughly embedded in the present. The Safavids did not merely rule Iran. They invented a version of it that the Qajars inherited, the Pahlavis restyled, the revolutionaries of 1979 weaponized, and the Islamic Republic still defends. Borders, faith, language, taste, grievance, pride - the crimson crown left fingerprints on each. To understand why Iran today looks and thinks and prays the way it does, one has to follow those fingerprints back to Tabriz, Qazvin, and above all to Isfahan. What follows traces what survived the fall.

Inventing Iran: Borders and National Identity

Before 1501, "Iran" was a cultural memory more than a political fact. The Persian-speaking world stretched from Anatolia to Bengal, ruled by Turks and Mongols who had absorbed Persian as the language of administration and verse. No single state called itself Iranian, answered to a shah in a capital, or drew a hard line around a recognizable territory. Shah Ismail changed that.

When his Qizilbash cavalry overran Tabriz and he declared himself shah, Ismail inherited the idea of Iran and fused it to a state. His heirs defended that state against enemies on every frontier, and in doing so they drew the outline that the modern map still recognizes. The Battle of Chaldoran in 1514, though a tactical disaster for Ismail, performed an unintended service: it froze the Safavid-Ottoman frontier roughly where it has remained ever since. The line separating Shi'i Iran from Sunni Turkey and Iraq is, in its deepest logic, a sixteenth-century line.

To the east, Safavid armies pushed back against Uzbek incursions into Khorasan. To the north and south, the Caspian coast and the Persian Gulf ports defined a state with coherent geography. When European diplomats of the seventeenth century spoke of "Persia," they meant the Safavid realm - a polity with a capital, a currency, a court, and a creed.

That coherence mattered because Iran, then as now, was not ethnically uniform. Turks, Persians, Kurds, Arabs, Armenians, Georgians, Lurs, Baluch, and Turkmen all lived under the shah. The genius of the Safavid project was to bind them together not by language - the court itself was bilingual, Turkic and Persian - but by two shared loyalties: to the person of the shah and to the Twelver faith he championed. A Kurdish tribesman and a Persian bureaucrat might share neither tongue nor custom, but they shared a qibla and an imam.

This was something new. Earlier Iranian empires, from the Sasanians to the Timurids, had ruled multiethnic populations, but none had constructed so self-conscious a fusion of territory, creed, and dynasty. The Safavids gave Iran a body.

When the dynasty fell, the body remained. Nader Shah tried to undo the religious settlement and failed. The Qajars who emerged in the late eighteenth century ruled a smaller, weaker Iran - but an Iran nonetheless, recognizable on the same map, praying in the same mosques, looking back to the same Isfahani golden age. Even the humiliations of the nineteenth century - the loss of the Caucasus to

Russia, the amputation of Herat - were measured against a Safavid baseline that every Iranian took for granted.

Modern Iranian nationalism, when it emerged in the twentieth century, had raw material to work with precisely because the Safavids had supplied it. Reza Shah Pahlavi's project of centralization, Mohammad Mosaddeq's defense of sovereignty, even the Islamic Republic's insistence on the indivisibility of its territory - all rest on a framework the Safavids built. The shape of Iran is their gift, and their imposition.

The Clerical Class and the Road to 1979

Of everything the Safavids bequeathed, the most consequential was also the least visible at the time: a clerical establishment with its own income, its own hierarchy, and its own claim to represent the Hidden Imam in his absence.

When Ismail declared Twelver Shi'ism the state religion in 1501, Iran had few Shi'i scholars. He imported them - from Jabal Amil in Lebanon, from Bahrain, from the shrine cities of Iraq. His successors endowed them with land, salaries, and institutional standing. By the reign of Shah Abbas, a network of seminaries, preachers, and judges had taken root, and Shi'i legal scholarship flourished in Isfahan and Qom as never before.

What made this clergy different from the Sunni ulama of the Ottoman lands was its structural independence. Sunni scholars were, in practice, civil servants of the sultan. Shi'i jurists, by contrast, derived their authority from the Hidden Imam - not from the shah. They collected their own religious taxes, the khums, directly from believers. They trained their own successors. They issued rulings that no king could simply overrule without incurring the charge of impiety.

The Safavid shahs tolerated this independence, even encouraged it, because the clergy legitimized their rule. But they also planted a rival. Figures like Muhammad Baqir Majlisi, the immensely powerful

Shaykh al-Islam of Isfahan under the last strong Safavid rulers, wielded an influence that shadowed the throne itself. When a later shah was weak, the clerics grew strong. When a later shah tried to reform, the clerics could obstruct.

That pattern did not end with the dynasty. Through the Qajar century, the ulama repeatedly checked royal power. They led the Tobacco Protest of 1891, forcing the shah to cancel a concession to a British company by declaring tobacco use forbidden until the deal was revoked - an entire nation obeyed the clergy over the crown. They played central roles in the Constitutional Revolution of 1906. Each time, they drew on a reservoir of moral authority and financial independence that traced straight back to the Safavid settlement.

Ayatollah Khomeini's revolution in 1979 was therefore not a rupture with Iranian history. It was the culmination of a long argument running since Shah Tahmasp invited foreign jurists to stock his mosques. Khomeini's doctrine of *velayat-e faqih* - the guardianship of the jurist - pushed the logic further than any Safavid cleric would have dared: the jurist was not merely the shah's advisor but his replacement. Yet the raw materials of that doctrine - an organized clergy, independent finances, a claim to speak for the Imam, a tradition of confronting unjust rulers - were all Safavid in origin.

Historians differ on how direct the line actually runs. Some argue that the activist political clergy of the twentieth century represented a sharp break with the quietist tradition of earlier centuries. Others see an unbroken thread. What is not in dispute is that without the Safavid decision to make Iran Shi'i, and to build the institutions that sustained that choice, there would be no Islamic Republic to argue about. Ismail's teenage declaration echoes, still, in every Friday sermon broadcast from Tehran.

The twelve folds of the crimson crown, once worn by Qizilbash warriors, are now embroidered into the black turbans of the men who run the country. They would not have it otherwise.

Persian as a World Literary Language

The Safavids inherited Persian literature; they did not invent it. Ferdowsi, Rumi, Hafez, Sa'di - all had done their work centuries before Ismail. What the Safavids did was something equally important: they curated, preserved, and universalized the Persian canon at precisely the moment when it might otherwise have dissolved into regional fragments.

Under Shah Tahmasp, the royal workshop produced the *Shahnameh* of Shah Tahmasp, one of the most lavishly illustrated manuscripts ever made. Every miniature was a statement: this is our epic, these are our kings, this language belongs to us. The shah later gave the manuscript as a diplomatic gift to the Ottoman sultan - a polite reminder, in paint and gold leaf, of whose cultural patrimony was whose.

Persian in the Safavid era was not confined to Iran. It was the working language of the Mughal court in Delhi, of administration across Central Asia, of trade from the Bosphorus to the Bay of Bengal. A merchant in Bukhara, a poet in Lahore, and a scribe in Istanbul could all correspond in Persian and understand each other perfectly. Safavid cultivation of Persian at the state level helped keep that lingua franca alive. Iranian poets emigrated to Mughal India in such numbers that historians speak of an "Indian style" (*sabk-e Hindi*) that dominated seventeenth-century verse across both empires.

Calligraphy reached new heights. The *nasta'liq* script, perfected by masters like Mir Ali Tabrizi before the Safavids and elevated further under their patronage, became the visual signature of Persian high culture. It still is. Any Iranian wedding invitation, any book of poetry on sale in a Tehran bookshop, any street sign rendered in decorative calligraphy carries forward a Safavid aesthetic.

Something subtler happened as well. By elevating certain authors and certain genres, the Safavid court helped fix what later generations would regard as classical. Hafez became the book found in every Iranian home, consulted for guidance on love and fate. Ferdowsi became the national poet, his thousand-year-old epic read as a charter of Iranian identity. These canonical statuses were not inevitable. They were curated, copied, illustrated, recited, and memorized under Safavid patronage until they became unquestionable.

When nineteenth-century European scholars began to translate Persian poetry - Goethe drawing on Hafez for his *West-östlicher Divan*, Edward FitzGerald remixing Omar Khayyam into English - they were working from texts and reputations consolidated during the Safavid centuries. The Persian literary tradition that entered world literature did so with a Safavid imprimatur.

Today, when an Iranian abroad recites Hafez from memory, or a calligrapher in Tehran shapes a line of Rumi in *nasta'liq*, or a tourist in Shiraz lays a rose on a poet's tomb, the transmission is unbroken. The language survived empires. The Safavids are a large reason why.

Memory and Nostalgia in Modern Iranian Culture

Every nation has a golden age it returns to in its imagination. For modern Iran, that age is Isfahan under Shah Abbas.

Naqsh-e Jahan Square - the "Image of the World" - still anchors the city. On its four sides sit the Shah Mosque, the Sheikh Lotfollah Mosque, the Ali Qapu Palace, and the entrance to the great bazaar. Built in the late sixteenth and early seventeenth centuries, the ensemble was conceived as a single composition: civic, commercial, royal, and religious power arranged in deliberate balance around an open field where polo was played and armies paraded. UNESCO inscribed it on the World Heritage list in 1979, the same year the revolution broke out. The dating is a coincidence, but a telling one. In the moment Iran was reinventing itself politically, the world was affirming the Safavid core of its cultural identity.

Iranians never needed the affirmation. The saying *Esfahan nesf-e jahan* - "Isfahan is half the world" - predates the revolution and will outlast it. It captures a pride that survives every regime change: whatever else has gone wrong, we built that.

Modern Iranian cinema returns again and again to the Safavid aesthetic. Historical dramas reconstruct the court of Shah Abbas. Contemporary architects quote the proportions of the Shah Mosque in buildings completed last year. Carpet designs produced today in workshops in Kashan and Tabriz still follow patterns codified under Safavid patronage. Miniature painting, ceramics, metalwork - the repertoire of what counts as "Persian" visual culture in a museum gift shop anywhere in the world was largely set in the Safavid ateliers.

Nostalgia can be political. The Pahlavi shahs, especially Mohammad Reza, staged extravagant ceremonies drawing on Safavid royal imagery to legitimize their own rule - less interested in the Shi'i content than in the grandeur of the form. The Islamic Republic reversed the emphasis, celebrating Safavid religious policy while downplaying courtly opulence. Both regimes claimed the inheritance. Neither could escape it.

Ordinary Iranians feel the pull in quieter ways. A family picnic on the grass of Naqsh-e Jahan. A grandfather explaining which dome was built first. A bride photographed in front of tilework four hundred years old. These are not the gestures of a people who treat their past as a museum. They are the gestures of a people still living in rooms their ancestors built.

Iranian cuisine, Iranian garden design, the Iranian sense of how a courtyard should feel with water running through it - all bear Safavid imprints. The past is not behind; it is underfoot.

Why the Safavids Belong in World History

World history as taught in the West has a Safavid-shaped hole. Students learn about the Ottomans, who menaced Vienna. They learn about the Mughals, who built the Taj Mahal. They learn about Ming and Qing China, about Tokugawa Japan, about the Habsburgs and the

Romanovs. The Safavids, squeezed between these giants on the map, are often reduced to a footnote: the empire Shah Abbas ruled, and something about carpets.

This is a serious distortion. The Safavid Empire was one of the great Islamic empires of the early modern era, a peer of the Ottomans and Mughals, and a key node in the global networks that defined the period from 1500 to 1700.

Consider the geography. Safavid Iran sat astride the overland routes between Europe, the Mediterranean, India, and China. Silk, the empire's signature export, flowed west through Aleppo and Izmir; silver flowed east in return. English and Dutch trading companies established factories at Bandar Abbas on the Persian Gulf, linking Iranian commerce to the wider maritime economy the Europeans were forging. When Shah Abbas drove the Portuguese from Hormuz in 1622 with English help, he was participating, as a full player, in the contest for control of the Indian Ocean.

Consider the religious dimension. By making Twelver Shi'ism a state project, the Safavids permanently altered the structure of the Muslim world. The Sunni-Shi'i divide shaping Middle Eastern politics today - from Baghdad to Beirut to Sanaa - took its modern form in the sixteenth century, in the confrontation between Istanbul and Isfahan. No honest account of global religious history can omit that chapter.

Consider the cultural exchanges. Armenian merchants from the Safavid suburb of New Julfa built trading houses as far as Amsterdam, Venice, and Madras. Jesuit missionaries debated theology at the court of Shah Abbas. European travelers - Jean-Baptiste Tavernier, Jean Chardin, Pietro della Valle - wrote accounts of Safavid Iran that shaped how Enlightenment Europe imagined the Orient. Voltaire and Montesquieu drew on these reports. The image of the wise, tolerant Persian in eighteenth-century European literature owes more to Isfahan than to any other source.

A tourist visiting Iran today, a diplomat negotiating with Tehran, a scholar reading a Khamenei speech, a worshipper in a Shi'i mosque from Lebanon to Pakistan - each is standing downstream of decisions made by shahs wearing the crimson crown. Few early modern empires can make that claim so directly.

The Safavids belong in world history because they shaped a world. Not just an Iranian world, though they did that most of all, but a connected one in which faith, art, and commerce flowed across frontiers they policed and frontiers they opened.

Quick Summary

- The Safavid Empire (1501-1736) gave Iran its modern shape: a coherent territory, a state religion in Twelver Shi'ism, and a national identity transcending ethnic divisions.

- The Battle of Chaldoran in 1514 froze the Iran-Turkey frontier in place; it has scarcely moved since.

- By importing and endowing a Shi'i clergy, the Safavids created an independent religious establishment whose descendants led the Tobacco Protest, the Constitutional Revolution, and ultimately the 1979 Islamic Revolution.

- Safavid patronage preserved and canonized Persian literature, calligraphy, and manuscript art, consolidating Persian as a world literary language used from Istanbul to Delhi.

- Isfahan under Shah Abbas remains the imagined golden age of Iranian culture, its monuments still defining "Persian" aesthetics globally.

- Safavid Iran was a full participant in the early modern global economy, trading silk for silver and negotiating with European powers in the Indian Ocean.

- The Sunni-Shi'i geopolitical divide shaping the modern Middle East took its recognizable form in the Safavid-Ottoman confrontation.

- Both the Pahlavi monarchy and the Islamic Republic have drawn legitimacy from competing readings of the Safavid inheritance.

The crimson crown was buried with the last weak shah in 1736, but its twelve folds were never really interred. They live in the borders on every map of Iran, in the cadences of every Persian poem memorized by heart, in the tilework of every mosque dome, and in the arguments of every jurist claiming to speak for the Hidden Imam. Empires are measured not by how long they last but by how long their logic outlasts them. By that measure, the Safavids are still ruling.

Empires are measured by how long their logic outlasts them, and by that measure the Safavids are still ruling. But the confidence with which one can say so depends on how much can actually be known about a dynasty whose own records were scattered by the Afghan sack of 1722. The picture assembled in these chapters rests on court chronicles, merchant ledgers, miniatures in distant museums, and stones still standing in Isfahan. How those fragments are gathered, weighed, and argued over is itself part of the Safavid story, and it is worth a closing look at the evidence behind the claims.

Note on Sources:

How We Know What We Know

The Safavid story survives in chronicles by court historians, account books of Dutch merchants, miniatures in scattered museums, and the worn stones of Isfahan itself. Reconstructing it is an act of patient triangulation.

No single archive holds the Safavid past. The dynasty's own records were scattered by the Afghan sack of Isfahan in 1722, and what court documentation survived was dispersed among successor regimes, private libraries, and eventually European collections. The historian working on this period must therefore move between Persian court chronicles, European travelers' memoirs, commercial ledgers in Dutch and English, Armenian merchant correspondence, Ottoman diplomatic files, and the material evidence of architecture, coinage, and painting. Each source has its silences. Court historians praised their patrons and slid past defeats. European visitors misread what they saw. Merchants cared about margins, not metaphysics. The picture that follows is the product of cross-checking all of them.

On Methodology

The spine of Safavid history is built from Persian-language chronicles written at or near the court. Works such as Amini Haravi's early narrative of Shah Ismail's rise, and the long series of dynastic histories composed under Tahmasp, Abbas, and their successors, supply the names, dates, campaigns, and genealogies on which everything else hangs. They are indispensable and also deeply partisan. A chronicler employed by a shah was not writing to puzzle future scholars; he was writing to justify a reign, flatter a patron, and place current events inside a providential frame in which the Safavid house was the rightful instrument of the Hidden Imam.

Reading these texts critically means noting what they omit as much as what they say. Defeats shrink to a paragraph. Inconvenient relatives vanish. Battles that the shah lost become strategic withdrawals. Court intrigues emerge only when a later regime finds it useful to expose them. The modern historian learns to read between the lines of elaborate Persian prose, cross-referencing claims against independent evidence wherever possible.

That independent evidence comes, above all, from Europeans. From the early sixteenth century onward, a steady stream of Portuguese, Italian, English, French, Dutch, and German visitors left accounts of what they saw in Iran. Some were ambassadors, some missionaries, some physicians, many were merchants. Jean Chardin, the French Huguenot jeweler who spent much of the 1670s in Isfahan, produced what remains the single richest description of late Safavid society, from court ceremonial to street markets to provincial administration. Engelbert Kaempfer, a German doctor attached to a Swedish embassy in the 1680s, wrote with the precision of a trained naturalist. Earlier travelers like Pietro della Valle and the Sherley brothers offer glimpses of Abbas's court at its zenith.

These outsiders are valuable because they noticed things the court historians took for granted - the prices of bread, the layout of bazaars, the behavior of eunuchs, the running of the royal harem - and because they had no stake in flattering the shah. But they carry their own distortions. Most did not read Persian well. They relied on interpreters with their own agendas. They sometimes mistook court gossip for fact, and they consistently misunderstood Shi'i theology. Used carefully, however, their accounts turn the chronicles from a monologue into a conversation.

The third leg of the tripod is commercial. The archives of the Dutch East India Company (VOC) and the English East India Company preserve thousands of letters and ledgers from factors stationed at Bandar Abbas, Isfahan, and elsewhere. Scholars like Willem Floor and Rudi Matthee have mined these papers to reconstruct the silk trade, currency flows, and the empire's entanglement with global capitalism. Armenian merchant correspondence from New Julfa, surviving in scattered family archives from Venice to Madras, adds another dimension, showing a diaspora that moved Persian silk from Isfahan to Amsterdam and, after the crisis years, resettled parts of its network in Europe.

Material culture fills gaps that texts leave open. Isfahan's surviving monuments - the Maidan, the Masjid-i Shah, the Ali Qapu, the bridges of Allahverdi Khan and Khaju - are primary sources in stone and tile. Safavid miniature paintings, now in the Topkapi, the British Library, the Metropolitan Museum, and private collections, encode political ideology, sartorial fashion, and notions of beauty. Carpets, ceramics, metalwork, and coins carry their own information about trade routes, workshop organization, and imperial self-image.

A final caution is conceptual. Safavid writers did not think of themselves as ruling a nation called Iran in the modern sense. Their categories - the Guarded Domains, the realm of the Shah, the lands of Islam - do not map neatly onto today's borders or identities. Good history of the period resists the temptation to read backward from the present.

Chronology

- **1252** - Sheikh Safi al-Din, eponym of the dynasty, is born in Ardabil.

- **1334** - Death of Sheikh Safi; the Safaviyya Sufi order continues under his descendants.

- **1487** - Ismail, future founder of the empire, is born in Ardabil.

- **1501** - Ismail captures Tabriz, declares himself Shah, and proclaims Twelver Shi'ism the state religion.

- **1510** - Ismail defeats and kills the Uzbek leader Muhammad Shaybani at the Battle of Marv.

- **1514** - Ottoman Sultan Selim I crushes Ismail at the Battle of Chaldiran.

- **1524** - Ismail dies; his ten-year-old son Tahmasp inherits a shaken empire.

- **1548** - Tahmasp moves the Safavid capital from Tabriz to Qazvin.

- **1555** - The Peace of Amasya establishes a long truce with the Ottomans.

- **1576** - Death of Tahmasp begins a decade of civil war and instability.

- **1587** - Shah Abbas I takes the throne in a coup at Qazvin.

- **1590** - Abbas signs a humiliating peace with the Ottomans to free his hands in the east.

- **1598** - Abbas defeats the Uzbeks and moves his capital to Isfahan.

- **1604** - Abbas forcibly relocates Armenian merchants from Julfa to a new suburb of Isfahan.

- **1622** - Anglo-Safavid forces expel the Portuguese from Hormuz.

- **1629** - Death of Shah Abbas the Great.

- **1639** - Treaty of Zuhab fixes the Ottoman-Safavid border roughly along today's Iran-Iraq line.

- **1666** - Accession of Shah Sulayman, beginning the era of harem-raised rulers.

- **1694** - Sultan Husayn, last effective Safavid shah, comes to the throne.

- **1709** - The Ghilzai Afghans revolt at Kandahar under Mir Wais.

- **1722** - Mahmud Hotak defeats the Safavid army at Gulnabad and besieges Isfahan; Sultan Husayn surrenders the throne.

- **1729** - Nadir Quli expels the Afghans and restores Tahmasp II as a puppet shah.

- **1736** - Nadir Shah is crowned at Mughan, formally ending the Safavid dynasty.

Further Reading

- **Andrew J. Newman, Safavid Iran: Rebirth of a Persian Empire (2006).** The single best scholarly synthesis of the dynasty in English, balanced and accessible.

- **Roger Savory, Iran Under the Safavids (1980).** A foundational survey by the leading Anglophone Safavid historian of the twentieth century.

- **Rudi Matthee, Persia in Crisis: Safavid Decline and the Fall of Isfahan (2012).** The definitive analysis of how and why the empire collapsed in 1722.

- **Rudi Matthee, The Politics of Trade in Safavid Iran: Silk for Silver, 1600-1730 (1999).** Essential for understanding the empire's place in the early modern global economy.

- **Kathryn Babayan, Mystics, Monarchs, and Messiahs: Cultural Landscapes of Early Modern Iran (2002).** A brilliant account of the religious and cultural transformations from Sufi mysticism to clerical Shi'ism.

- **Sussan Babaie, Isfahan and Its Palaces: Statecraft, Shi'ism, and the Architecture of Conviviality (2008).**

Beautifully illustrated study of the capital's monuments as expressions of imperial ideology.

- **Sheila Canby, Shah 'Abbas: The Remaking of Iran (2009).** Catalogue of a major British Museum exhibition, lavishly illustrated and authoritative.

- **Sheila Canby, The Golden Age of Persian Art, 1501-1722 (1999).** The standard introduction to Safavid painting, manuscripts, and decorative arts.

- **Jean Chardin, Travels in Persia, 1673-1677 (1711).** The richest European eyewitness account of late Safavid Iran, indispensable to all later historians.

- **Engelbert Kaempfer, Am Hofe des persischen Grosskonigs, 1684-1685 (1712).** A German physician's careful observations of the Safavid court, recently translated and reissued.

- **Colin P. Mitchell, The Practice of Politics in Safavid Iran: Power, Religion and Rhetoric (2009).** Innovative study of how language and chancery practice constructed Safavid authority.

- **Willem Floor, Safavid Government Institutions (2001).** Detailed reference work on the bureaucratic machinery of the empire.

- **Said Amir Arjomand, The Shadow of God and the Hidden Imam (1984).** Classic sociological study of how Shi'ism became fused with Iranian statehood.

- **David Blow, Shah Abbas: The Ruthless King Who Became an Iranian Legend (2009).** A readable, narrative-driven biography for the general reader.

- **Hans Robert Roemer, The Safavid Period (in The Cambridge History of Iran, vol. 6) (1986).** The standard reference chapter, dense but comprehensive.

Two and a half centuries of Safavid rule rest, in the end, on a fragile web of evidence: a chronicler's phrase, a merchant's ledger entry, a traveler's sketch, a tile still clinging to a dome in Isfahan. Historians keep returning to this period because the puzzle is genuinely unfinished. New manuscripts surface in regional libraries. Digitization is opening Armenian and Georgian archives long sealed to outsiders. Archaeological work in Ardabil and on the Persian Gulf coast continues to revise what had seemed settled. The Safavid empire that forged modern Iran is still coming into focus, and the picture will look different again a generation from now.